SUCCESS WITH
FINISHING

DATE DUE	

GAYLORD   PRINTED IN U.S.A.

SUCCESS WITH
FINISHING

MARK CASS

GUILD OF MASTER CRAFTSMAN PUBLICATIONS LTD

For Mira, Alex and Marcus

First published 2006 by
Guild of Master Craftsman Publications Ltd,
166 High Street, Lewes,
East Sussex BN7 1XU

ISBN 1 86108 426 9
A catalogue record of this book is available from the British Library.

Production Manager: Hilary MacCallum
Managing Editor: Gerrie Purcell
Editor: Rachel Netherwood
Managing Art Editor: Gilda Pacitti
Photography: Anthony Bailey, Mark Cass
Book design: John Hawkins

Typefaces: Palatino and Frutiger

Colour origination: Altaimage
Printed and bound: Sino Publishing

Contents

Introduction

Welcome to another in the 'Success with' series of books. After reading this one you should have a much better idea of how to achieve a professional finish for your woodwork, as well as having a greater understanding of the many different products, techniques and processes involved. It's best to look upon the advice offered here as 'steps towards' success. A certain amount of patience will be required as success is really something to be achieved through hard work, practice and application, and is only occasionally encountered in finishing by luck and good fortune.

It's not my intention to blind you with science and unnecessary facts within these pages, but certain chemical and physical reactions are a vital part of good finishing and cannot be ignored, so pay attention at the back there!

Like many other skilled crafts, polishing (the catch-all term to describe the application of nearly all furniture finishes), as practised by a professional and viewed by the novice, can take on an air of mysterious alchemy, especially when glimpsed in a dingy or cavern-like workshop. All the bottles, jars, tins and boxes arranged on shelves around the room, each one encrusted with years of built-up polish, varnish and wax, seem to add to the air of impenetrable masonry or some other secret society.

As an outsider just passing by and looking in, you have little chance of getting the artisan within to divulge many secrets, but if he or she is in good humour, you may be permitted to watch quietly for a while. I would recommend such a course of action, for much can be learned by observation and there are many things that can't be effectively described by mere words.

Good finishing is, however, achievable by anyone with simple equipment and a modest kit of supplies, as long as the basic principles of preparation and application are adhered to, and sufficient trouble is taken to execute each step diligently and in a professional manner. You really need to be thorough in all aspects of your work, and resist the temptation to take shortcuts until you have a fuller understanding of the procedures and processes involved.

So, if you're fully prepared for some hard work, the occasional set-back, and a fair bit of frustration, take a deep breath, enter the world of spirit stains, oil-based varnish, lacquers and wax, and read on.

Top quality furniture demands a top quality finish – just don't choose something like this to practise on.

A professional workshop often holds a special atmosphere, and it's not just down to the fumes, either.

Part 1:
Getting started

1.1 Overview

When I first started making things out of wood, a finish of any kind represented only an annoying delay to using (or, as a boy, playing with) the latest creation, and consequently it was rushed through in a fit of impatience. As the years have passed, I've stopped thinking like this and have come to realize that finishing is just one more, equally important, aspect of the complete job. Once you make this mental step, preparing for and applying your selected finish isn't an inconvenience to be grudgingly gone through with, but becomes an acceptable, enjoyable part of the project.

Base basics

One of the most important things to know when applying finishes is the distinction between the bases of different products. There are spirit-based finishes, those based on oils, and the newer acrylic or water-based ones. Put simply, the base of a product is the solvent or liquid the various 'finish' components are dissolved in or mixed with, and will be the same as that used for cleaning your brushes or other equipment. An example of a spirit-based finish would be French polish; an oil-based product could be a varnish; and a water-based finish might be an acrylic floor sealer. See the table on page 15 for the base compatibility of each product.

> **KEY POINT**
>
> Whenever a finish is applied over a similarly based previous coat, there is often the possibility that the second will partially dissolve the first. In some cases making sure that the first coat is fully dry will help avoid this, and in other cases a sealing coat between the two will prevent it from happening. Either way, some vigilance is called for and samples should be made up wherever possible to ascertain what will work or not.

Spray lacquer is an example of the fourth base – nitrocellulose.

ⓕFOCUS ON:

Base compatibility

Product	Base compatibility	Description
Ethanol	Spirit	Pure alcohol; will readily dissolve shellac
Methanol	Spirit	Alcohol with added poison, often referred to as 'denatured'
Methylated spirits	Spirit	Similar to methanol but with added dye
White spirits	Oil	Extracted from the upper refinery streams during the fractional distillation of crude oil. Sometimes known as mineral spirits
Naphtha	Oil	Similar to white spirits; also a good general purpose solvent
Turpentine	Oil	An effective solvent for oil-based paints and varnishes, derived from pine trees
Acetone	Cellulose	A manufactured chemical that also occurs naturally. Highly evaporative, organic solvent
Thinners	Cellulose	General term; usually in reference to cellulose spray finishes
Acrylic	Water	Increasingly popular finish base; least harmful to the environment

Finish types

Reactive	These harden by reaction with air or other substances (such as a chemical catalyst). Once hardened, no reverse is possible. Varnish is a good example.
Evaporative	These dry by evaporation with no polymerization (molecular bonding) taking place. They can be re-dissolved by their solvent – such as shellac (French polish) and some lacquers – at any time.

The four bases: oil, spirit, water and cellulose.

Trust your nose.

Popular finishes

Varnish

This is possibly the most familiar of all wood finishes, and undoubtedly the most misunderstood and abused. Varnish was initially developed by seafarers as a waterproofing agent for their boats, in a time when good use was made of everything that a tree could offer – not just the timber, but also the resin which seeped slowly from within.

Varnish has been used on boats for centuries.

Varnishes are generally made up of four component parts: resin, oil, spirit and driers. The resin is the part of the varnish that forms the hard film, and the spirit, often turpentine, is what it's dissolved in. The oil – linseed or tung, for example – provides a bit of flexibility and elasticity to the varnish while the driers speed up the drying time, which is very important, especially in today's busy world. After application, the oil in the varnish slowly dries, absorbing oxygen and becoming a tough and slightly pliable solid, helped by the evaporation of the spirit content and a subtle polymerization of the resin. While oil-based varnishes are still popular with restorers and musical instrument makers, most of us will be familiar with today's synthetic version: polyurethane. Although they are more hard-wearing, polyurethane varnishes can have a 'plastic' appearance, and are harder to repair when damaged than the oil-based equivalents.

Easily applied, varnish is a good all-rounder.

There are also spirit-based varnishes, which are similar to oil varnishes except that the resin is dissolved in alcohol – generally ethanol – and used in one or two specialist applications, notably for knotting prior to painting. Water-based varnishes are now available as a result of continuing demand for safer and more environmentally friendly products, and these are steadily improving in quality and durability all the time.

Varnish is ideal for interior woodwork.

French polish

This is the classic furniture finish, the one which gives many antiques their special and desirable appearance. It is achievable in varying degrees of quality by the amateur but, when mastered, it really is an impressive skill – something that soon becomes apparent when watching the professional at work and the results produced.

French polish is made from shellac, a powdered insect-derived resin, which is dissolved in spirit or alcohol – however unlikely that sounds in today's hi-tech world. Developed in France in the 1820s, French polishing has been popular ever since, as its matchless high sheen is still sought after by many discerning customers today.

Unlike most other finishes, French polish is applied with a cotton pad or polishing 'rubber', which is used to produce the beautiful high lustre most of us are familiar with. Unfortunately it's not the most hard-wearing or durable of finishes and is easily marked by solvents, alcohol or water – so perhaps it might not be the most suitable finish for your new bar-top.

This Art Deco table is enhanced by shellac.

French polishing is a satisfying 'hands on' affair.

Wax

Wax is probably the oldest and most widely used of finishes, and for centuries has remained a popular and pleasing finish for all things made of wood. Despite offering little in the way of protection, a wax finish built up over the years is particularly appealing, something that the patient amongst us will appreciate more than others.

Most commonly used as a sacrificial or maintenance finish over a shellac or a varnish, wax is great for giving an instant 'lift' to a tired finish, as well as imparting the local atmosphere with one of the nicest smells known to mankind.

The majority of paste waxes are formulated from carnauba, beeswax and paraffin wax. The carnauba, a palm tree derivative, gives a wax its hardness and shine; beeswax is softer and has a more satiny appearance; and paraffin is added to make the wax more easy to apply. Coloured pigments and dyes are often added, and their use is to be encouraged, especially on darker woods, or else an inadvertent liming effect could occur.

The most notable exception to the general make-up of a furniture wax is a proprietary brand known as Briwax. This has a different smell and constituency to most waxes, having a higher toluene content than other similar products. Unlike the majority of paste waxes, Briwax needs to be buffed up immediately after application and builds up a 'skin' in a very short time. It is most effective on pine and has long been a staple of the antique pine furniture trade.

Original beeswax remains popular today.

Coloured Briwax can rapidly change the appearance.

Well-maintained wax finishes always improve with age.

Lacquered finishes are the mainstay of factory-produced furniture.

Cellulose lacquer

This is another misunderstood finish, mainly used in mass production and factory-assembled furniture. Developed as an alternative to shellac in the 1920s, its main constituent is cellulose nitrate (commonly known as nitrocellulose), and was produced from post-war gun cotton stockpiles in its early days.

As time has gone by, additives and continued developments have improved the characteristics of this hard-wearing finish, and it is now widely used throughout the world, despite its sometimes slightly suspect 'ageing' characteristics. It can look shabby quite quickly if abused and neglected.

For the amateur woodworker, cellulose lacquer won't be the first finish on the list. It is almost exclusively applied by spray gun, and is only really viable for batch production; both the cost of materials and the effort involved in setting up a spray booth make it rarely cost effective for smaller work.

Turned work is well suited to an oiled finish.

Oil

Oil finishes are increasingly popular these days, partly due to their subtle semi-matt appearance, and also because they must be one of the easiest finishes to apply without too much fear of ruining the job. They are especially convenient for smaller work, particularly carving or turnings.

Derived from natural constituents, linseed, tung and Scandinavian are among some of the most commonly available oils. They are all examples of 'drying' oils, which means that they will harden and dry when exposed to oxygen, unlike, for instance, a mineral oil that you would use on your oilstone. This is obviously an important characteristic for woodworkers, as well as the oil's ability to add depth and enhance the figure of the timber. Many years ago the craftsman would produce a special, deep lustre oil finish with daily application of linseed oil rubbed in by hand, generally for weeks, sometimes even for months.

Kitchen worktops stay looking good with regular oiling.

Environmentally safe finishes are much in demand today.

Acrylic varnishes provide a food-safe finish.

Water-based finishes

Acrylics were originally developed as a safe and environmentally friendly alternative to cellulose finishes, but the early water-based lacquers and seals were not entirely successful, tending to mark quite easily and to react poorly to water and steam. Now, however, it's a different story and water-based finishes are right up there with their longer-established chemical counterparts.

As it becomes more difficult to legally spray cellulose and solvent-based finishes in towns and built-up areas, professionals are increasingly looking towards less toxic options. Water-based finishes fill this need, as well as being considerably less harmful to the environment. They are also non-flammable, and very popular with the occasional or DIY finisher who likes the easy clean-up and lack of odour.

Because water is not a solvent for most resins, other chemicals are added to create and maintain an emulsion of evenly dispersed resin in the mainly water liquid carrier. These other chemicals help give the acrylic finish its distinctive blue-white colour, something that can be an advantage when finishing

Non-toxic paints are a must for children's toys.

white or light-coloured timbers where maintaining their natural colour is important.

Water-based finishes take a bit of getting used to at first, especially if you're used to the golden hue that most other solvent-based finishes impart, but advantages such as short drying times, ease of application and a fume-free environment soon outweigh their shortcomings.

Colourless acrylic seals are the perfect treatment for light, modern floors.

Floor sealers

These finishes represent quite a specialized field of their own; they are developed to provide the hardest-wearing finish of all, as well as enhancing the looks of the timber floor they're applied to.

The strongest and most hard-wearing of floor seals have traditionally been oil-based. These tend to have a timber-enhancing golden hue to them, and usually require a minimum of 12 to 24 hours between coats. This is fine if the floor is in a corporate boardroom which is empty over the weekend, but close to impractical if it's your front room the day before a party.

For a few years now, acrylic seals have been gaining popularity both in the trade and for the switched-on DIY finisher. Their hard-wearing characteristics are generally on par with the oil-based equivalents, although they won't add anything much in the way of colour, possessing the familiar milky tone common to most acrylic finishes.

Wax can play a part in a floor finish, although mainly in a maintenance capacity, both on oil- and water-based seals. Oiled finishes by themselves are finding increased popularity; a simple matt to satin effect is generally the result, although regular applications are required to keep the floor protected and looking good.

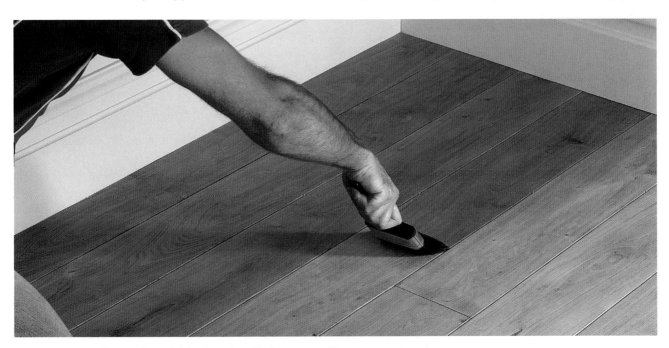

Time taken in applying a floor finish correctly will always pay off.

Paint

This remains as popular a finish as ever, and while not quite in the same field as polishes and varnishes, can't really be overlooked in a book on finishes. There is always a place for paint in the woodwork world; not all projects lend themselves to exotic hardwoods and sometimes the unifying qualities of a single colour are just the thing to disguise an unsightly mix of woods and man-made boards. Things are a lot easier for today's consumer: any colour you choose can be mixed to your exact specifications, and in any type or finish that you desire. This is a far cry from less than a hundred years ago, when painting and decorating were the exclusive reserve of the professional, and raw pigments and stains were mixed on site in less than ideal conditions.

A good paint finish is readily achievable by the home woodworker, but certain guidelines have to be followed, together with diligent preparation, to give your work that professional appearance which sets it apart from the rushed, amateur look that a lot of us will be sadly familiar with.

A professional painter knows that careful preparation really pays off.

Only a basic tool kit is needed to obtain first-class results.

Special finishes

There are a number of finishes that don't really fall into any of the previous categories, but are well worth a mention here. Some of these finishes, for instance stencilling and various paint effects, come and go like high-street fashions.

Ebonizing was very popular in the late 19th and early 20th centuries. It involves a jet-black and polished finish applied to a close-grained timber to resemble ebony, an expensive and scarce exotic. It still has a place in furniture making today, especially when used as a contrast or accent with blond or gold-coloured woods and veneers.

Fumed oak has long been a staple of British furniture and was originally employed to emulate the age-darkened hues of medieval pieces. Ammonia is the active ingredient in this process, its powerful fumes reacting with oak to progressively darken it over the course of a few hours.

Hand-applied details – the ultimate decoration.

An ebonized finish – classier than black paint.

Gilding is a very specialized finish indeed, and is something I will be attempting to describe here, although personal tuition from a professional is recommended for the novice. Pure metals, most notably gold, are hammered into sheets of an extraordinary thinness. These expensive sheets are applied with great care using delicate brushes to decorative carvings, picture frames or even complete pieces of furniture.

Stencils are one of those finishes that come and go. There is a small place for this sort of thing, and if used with care, the addition of a stencilled symbol or motif repeated discreetly on one or two items of complementary furniture can be effective. Decoupage – applied pictures or text from magazines, posters or other media – is a cheap and interesting solution to giving a fresh lease of life to an otherwise bin-worthy item. It was very popular in the late 19th century, particularly on screens and room dividers.

One of the most popular and enduring of finishes is authentic age. For the last few decades crafts people have striven to replicate the beautiful and hard-worn patinas of genuine antiques. Passable efforts are achievable with a lot of time and hard work.

Like most things, moderation is the key for a special finish to really work and look good on a job. If you're not careful, you can start to get carried away by your success and keep repeating the effect around the house, and before you know it, the overall effect is considerably lessened.

See the table on pages 166–168 for details of what finishes are best suited for most of the popular timbers and man-made boards available today. And remember: if in doubt, try it out.

1.2 Preparation

Ask any professional, be they painter or polisher, and they will tell you that good preparation is paramount to a successful finish. It is a cliché I know, but for very good reason. If you want your work to be something to be proud of, to be passed down through the generations, then you should be looking to make it as good as you can in every respect. Once you adopt this philosophy, you'll find yourself striving for perfection more often than you might expect. The very fact that you're reading this book implies that you want more from your work than just the cheap shine from a coat or two of budget polyurethane.

Preparation from new

Sanding is possibly the most important stage in the transformation from the bench-top prototype appearance to a fully finished piece of furniture you can be proud of. What you're looking for is a uniform smooth finish to every part of the work, with special care taken on the top or any other prominent areas. Basically, the smoother you can get your timber, the better the finish will be, not to mention the easier it will be to apply.

Large, flat areas like table tops present the biggest challenge, but if your joinery or cabinetry has been of a decent standard, it should be possible to get a good result. In the trade, belt sanders are the power tool of choice for the busy maker, although the best option of all would be an industrial speed sander.

An old finish should be thoroughly sanded down.

Time spent cleaning up a new piece will ensure a much better final result.

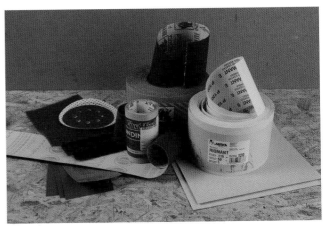
Sandpaper is available in a wide variety of grades and types.

Occasionally a job will stand the expense of hiring one of these, but for most of us the belt sander should be the first method to consider. For a novice, it's all too easy to let a belt sander get out of control, something which usually results in dips and gouges on the surface. While this won't be too obvious at the sanding stage, when you get some finish on the top, every contour will be only too apparent for all to see.

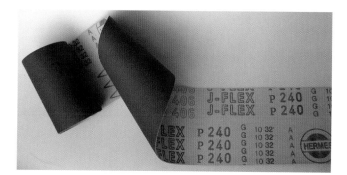

Flexible cloth-backed abrasive like this is ideally suited for mouldings and curved work.

A random orbital sander is the professional's choice.

Careful belt sanding will quickly prepare your flat surfaces.

The bigger and better belt sanders often have a frame accessory available which holds the sander perfectly level and ensures the sanding is flat and uniform, something which is definitely worth considering when you're looking to buy one.

Don't despair though, if you don't have access to a belt sander, because you can get perfectly acceptable results with a random orbital or even a humble orbital sander. Just don't make the mistake of using too coarse a paper at first, which means that you don't really want to start with anything less than 100 or 120. Keep the sander moving at all times, and let the tool do the work – you shouldn't have to press down

too hard. It's worth doing this in a well-ventilated area, preferably with your vacuum extractor attached and wearing a mask as well.

Work your way down through the grades, finishing off with 180 at the very least and make sure to work with the grain at all times. It's often easier to hand-sand the smaller parts of a job with paper and a cork or rubber block, and it's really worth paying close attention to any mouldings and other areas that will catch the light. You should be able to run your hands over any part of the work and not feel any sharp or rough edges at all. While you're having a final close inspection, make sure there are no traces of dried glue or filler smeared over the piece – a sharp chisel blade or scraper may be required here – as again, it might look OK now, but when the finish or stain goes on, these sorts of blemishes have a habit of jumping out at you and demanding your attention.

Preparation from old

Keep your eyes peeled for shabby or painted bargains.

Not all of us will start our finishing on pristine items of furniture fresh from the cabinet maker's workshop; something just waiting for a casual coating of oil to be rendered perfect. More often than not it will be a chair or table from a local junk shop which represents an ideal opportunity both to show off our 'restoration' skills and to get a nice piece of furniture into the house at a modest cost.

It's at this point that I have to airily instruct the reader to make sure the piece of furniture is fundamentally sound before starting work. Of course, we don't want to spend time and effort re-staining and finishing our piece only to have it collapse in a corner when the next door neighbour settles her sizeable frame into it. So, unless it's a piece of furniture you simply must have, regardless of its condition, spend a little extra time on inspection before you buy it.

At the risk of offending the shop-owner or stall-holder, don't be scared to look underneath your bargain, turning it over if possible, and generally subjecting it to some firm (but controlled) manipulation to ascertain how solid the item is. This is something that you only get better at with practice, so be prepared for a non-bargain or two in the early days.

Getting started

OK, so you've got your bargain home and you're in the shed or garden poised with the brush and stripper, ready to take it back to the wood. Just hold on a moment, do you really need to? It's possible that a light cleaning will be all that's required. If the finish is a bit tired and dirty, you can clean it up with a 'finish restoring' solution. This is something you can buy off the shelf, or make yourself with linseed oil and methylated spirits in a 50/50 solution. This should then be applied gently with a fine wire wool. Carefully try this out on a less visible part of the piece of furniture first, and see what happens. Very often it will soften old polish and spirit-based varnish, both removing dirt and preparing the surface for a new finish. If successful, you can proceed on to the rest of the surface, then leave it to dry for the next stage.

It's quite possible though, to encounter layers of chipped and flaking varnish which won't respond to your gentle efforts. If this is the case, then put into effect the original plan A. Remember, at this stage we're just exploring different ways to avoid total stripping, safe in the knowledge that we have this option to fall back on should it all go horribly wrong.

A finish-restoring solution is easily prepared.

Always try a reviver first – you may be pleasantly surprised.

KEY POINT

If you're trying to repair an old finish, it's important to use a similar product to that already there so as to keep the item looking reasonably authentic. As acrylic finishes have not been with us for long, it's a safe bet that your antique dining chair will have been finished with either spirit- or oil-based materials or that your 1950s kitchen table received a coating of nitrocellulose lacquer at the factory. If authenticity is not a big concern then it will be a job for the stripper after all.

A Georgian chest (with Victorian knobs) awaiting some TLC.

Stripping

Over the years I've seen some extraordinary sights emerge from under layers of paint, and this is one more reason to proceed with caution when first investigating. Even if you have decided to strip, still make sure to start on an out-of-the-way part of the piece until you have established just what is underneath. I was once fortunate and prudent enough to follow this course on a small Victorian occasional table. The top of the table had originally been painted as a display of faux-marble samples in stunning colours and variety, and I took great pleasure in gently removing the existing black finish (which turned out to be an ebonizing French polish) to expose the rich colours and awesome handiwork of a master decorator, and then returning the table to its astonished owner. It would have been a real shame if I'd steamed in with chemical stripper and a 4-inch scraper, plus I'd have missed out on my bonus.

Stripper makes use of an old brush.

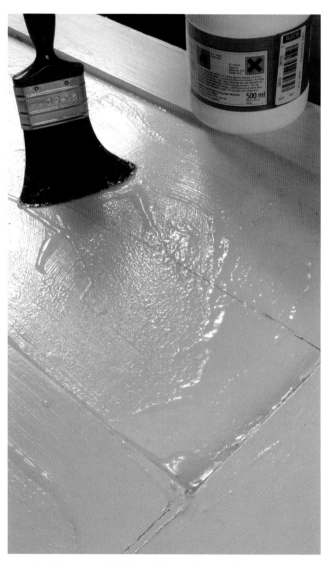

Lay the stripper on thickly and leave it to work.

Stripping is what apprentices were invented for, but a session or two should be compulsory for anyone working with wood and furniture just to make them appreciate how good the good jobs are. Don't even think of carrying out this messy task in your front room, even if you do put paper down. In my experience stripper gets everywhere and inevitably you'll find odd splashes in places you'd never expect. Remember, this is a caustic product that will damage everything it comes into contact with.

Outside is favourite, what with the fumes and all, but I happen to like a bench or table in the workshop with tools, rags and preferably a tap nearby. Old clothes are a must, and you can say goodbye to your new trainers if you don't remember to change them too. I expect I'm not the only one who has seen various items of furniture or woodwork in an unfinished, half-stripped condition in people's houses, often abandoned in the spare room or garage. This is because it's an unpleasant, dirty job, and one which often takes a lot longer than imagined. It shouldn't really be attempted in anything less than a fully confident spirit, but it is a job nonetheless that is hugely rewarding when finally completed.

Prepare yourself for a lengthy session, get in plenty of coarse wire wool, your preferred chemical stripper, rags and newspapers, and an old brush or two. A warped part of me actually enjoys this job because, once you're committed, you might as well go all out in a stripping frenzy and get the job over with as soon as possible.

Any type of scraping tool can be employed for this operation, although blunt is best.

KEY POINT

If you're stripping paint, this is a great opportunity to make good use of those brushes that are standing dried-up and hard as cricket bats in a cobwebbed jar in the corner of the workshop. Keep your fingers crossed that they're natural bristle because acrylic or polyester bristle will die. Pour out some stripper into a jar before you start and put them in to start 'soaking'. By the time you've got your work surface prepared (and the surrounding area cleared of anything you care about), found yourself some heavy-duty gloves and some eye protection, lined up your rolls of wire wool and the scissors to cut it, your brushes will be starting to soften up and you'll be ready for action.

A dedicated stripping area means better concentration on the job in hand.

ⓕ FOCUS ON:

Safety

Just a note here about gloves. My first stripping experiences were carried out in a pair of fetching pink rubber gloves – these are great for the washing up, but close to useless for paint stripping. Within minutes the finger tips go through, and this is when you find you just have to grin and bear the strange, cold burn that only paint stripper can bring. What you need are proper heavy-duty rubber gloves, but not only are these pricier, they are often just a bit too thick when it comes to dexterity, adding another level of difficulty to an already tricky job. However, if you value having a sense of touch for the next few days, not to mention smooth partner-friendly skin, then gloves really are advisable.

Eye protection is absolutely essential. Take it from me, when you get paint stripper in the eye it is scary and very unpleasant.

Eye and hand protection is a must – the other parts of you will just have to take their chances.

Use your brush to slop the stripper over the piece in a free and easy manner; try to restrict the working area to something approaching a manageable one (so don't try to do it all at once). Following the instructions on the tin, give it sufficient time to start working, then set to work with the wire wool. Some people like to use a metal scraper; if you use one, make sure it's blunt, to avoid damaging the work. I find the risk of damage, particularly when enveloped in a haze of chemicals and with restricted vision and burning fingers, is fairly high, so I prefer to stick to the slightly gentler, if more costly, method of wire wool.

I find a bit of music helps, as often a second, third or even fourth application is needed before all traces of paint are gone (along with a surprising amount of stripper, lots of wire wool and a fair amount of your best rags). On the upside though, not only have you successfully completed a difficult and dirty task, you've also got a clean and fresh piece of furniture in front of you and a 'back-from-the-dead' paintbrush or two, not to mention a healthy thirst for a restorative drink of your choice. Before you rush to the kitchen though, two more important tasks await: the whole job needs to be washed down with methylated spirits (if you're using a standard caustic stripper) or white spirit or water if you don't mind waiting a bit longer for it to dry. This is vitally important so that all the stripper residue is removed or neutralized before applying the new finish. Some fine or medium grade wire wool is good for this or else use some clean coarse cloth, preferably white or faded.

Finally, have a good tidy up, and be sure to collect all the old wire wool, rags and paper from the floor and work surface. It's best to leave a freshly stripped item overnight so it can thoroughly dry;

Be sure to check that your exquisite timber isn't just painted on, like this 'rosewood' on a beech chair.

if you're impatient and rush things there's every likelihood you'll get an unwanted reaction with your finish and consequently be wracked with regret for ever more. The next day, a close inspection is called for, and any residues of paint remaining in cracks, crevices or moulding can be carefully picked out with a sharp pointed stick. Finally, a light sanding down with a fine paper is a good idea, especially if water has been used at all.

Filling

Few professional woodworkers I know will admit to using much filler – in my experience it's usually kept under the bench or hidden in a cupboard somewhere out of sight in their workshop. It's a fact though, that for most of us a bit of filler is often the only way to get round a flaw or knot in the timber, or a chip of moulding that has accidentally disappeared.

If it can be avoided, it should be, especially if it's going to be in a prominent place on your job, because a patch of filler seems to draw the eye to it like the fake diamonds on a snide Rolex. Over the years I've developed my own methods for discreet repairs, and top of the list is trying to avoid the need for filler in the first place. Next down the list is remaking or replacing the damaged component. Obviously there are many factors to be taken into account here, but I would strongly recommend a bit more woodwork, even if it delays the job a little.

Two-part filler will often get you out of trouble, but be sure you use it with restraint.

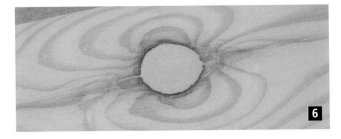

1 A fine pin or two will 'anchor' the filler.
2 Masking tape covers the back.
3 – **5** Filler is mixed, applied, then sanded down.
6 The finished repair – ready to paint or disguise.

(KEY POINT

If you're dealing with a dent in your timber, it may well be possible to fix it by steaming it out. Just apply a drop or two of water to the affected area, let it soak in for a bit, then gently apply a hot iron through a damp cloth to convert the water to steam which will swell the wood fibres back up to their original size and shape.

Wood stopping is an effective filler for pin and nail holes.

Otherwise, your eye will forever be drawn to your mistake every time you look at it. Machining out a bit of extra timber for emergencies at the start of a job is always a safe bet, and it's something I've never regretted doing.

If you do plan to go down the woodfiller route, try to get a colour that will come close to matching your final finished shade. There are plenty of coloured fillers available these days, or you can tint a neutral one using spirit powder stains (see chapter 2:1). One of the trickiest things to deal with are the holes left from pinning on a length of moulding. Despite their small size, a veneer pin or fine panel pin can be troublesome, especially at eye-level or in a long run somewhere. A stopping product such as Brummer is the usual method for dealing with small holes, but there's no guarantee that your stain or finish won't highlight the filled blemishes rather than hide them.

Again, a bit of experimentation is called for here, both with different types of stopping and with stains and finishes on the repaired holes. Of late I have had some success with coloured waxes. These are available in a nice range of colours (or you can even melt them down and mix your own if you have a double boiler. Be careful though, as there's plenty of scope for accidents here). Most importantly, these are applied at the end of the job when the final

colour and finish is apparent. For the improving woodworker I would say to try and avoid visible nails and pins wherever possible. Depending on what glue you use it's perfectly acceptable to hold mouldings and trim in place with clamps, masking tape or any device that can be removed later, leaving no mark.

Another common error, when left with a large dollop of filler, is to generously apply it to every tiny blemish, ding or scratch you can see. Not only is this a false economy (you're better off throwing your surplus filler away than using it unnecessarily), but you've given yourself a lot more sanding down to do. It's worth bearing in mind that you've also filled the grain surrounding each mark, something that will become dramatically apparent the moment you apply your finish. I've seen too many jobs spoiled this way so either be very sparing with the filler and careful how you apply it, or make sure you remove all of it from the surrounding area, whether by scraping, sanding or picking it out of the grain with something sharp.

Dust

After any preparation, whether on old or new furniture, the final thing needed is a good dusting down with a dust brush. This is not just for tidiness; it is essential in order to prevent contaminating the future finish, which is something that is sadly all too often encountered in rushed or careless work. After a dust off, you should employ the use of a tack cloth to make sure as much foreign matter as possible is removed. A tack cloth is simply a fine rag impregnated with some kind of sticky oil which won't affect a paint or varnish finish, and is often the quick and convenient solution (see chapter 2:8).

A wide variety of dust masks is available.

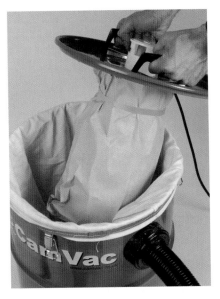

Triple-filtered extraction is desirable.

Grain filling

For a really superior finish, it's desirable to have all surfaces prepared to the utmost flatness, with barely a hint of grain detectable. A fine paste known as grain filler is employed for this purpose, which is basically a thinned-down filler, usually coloured to match your timber, and is rubbed into the grain and left to dry. Be careful not to use too much or you will make plenty of extra work for yourself in scraping and sanding it off. Once this has been sanded smooth you're on your way to what's known in the trade as a 'full-grain finish'.

Old-time polishers used plaster of Paris, vestiges of which can often be seen glowing faintly white in antique furniture of the early 20th century. It's not strictly necessary for the average job, but it will help you to obtain an easier shine on coarse or open-grained timbers.

Commercially available grain filler will create a flatter surface.

Sanding sealer

Often used as a cheap option by those on a tight budget, sanding sealer will give your work a bit of a shine, but its main use is that of a pre-finish. Designed to seal up the pores of your timber and to lock the wood fibres together, it is available in spirit- or oil-based versions for compatibility with the finish of your choice.

Varnish sanding sealer is an oil-based product, a thinned varnish mixed with zinc stearate, which is the same anti-clog agent used in the manufacture of sandpaper. The stearates give the first coat extra body, sand down easily and help the top coat go on with less effort.

KEY POINT

You can make your own sanding sealer by thinning your varnish 50/50 with white spirit or turpentine. As well as being a satisfying option, thinned varnish won't obscure the colour of your work and is particularly recommended for new wood that isn't naturally oily.

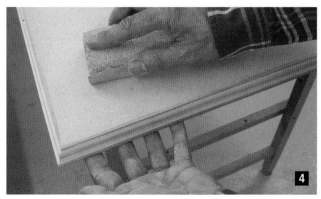

1 A freshly-machined MDF edge is highly absorbent.
2 Initial sanding should be thorough.
3 Sanding sealer is now applied and left to dry.
4 A final sanding leaves the work ready for its finish.

1:3 Safety

Who would have thought that a process that involves no power tools and little contact with a sharp blade, could be so potentially dangerous? Well, not me! That is, not until I nearly passed out from inhaling toxic fumes while working in a confined area.

Of course, there are plenty of potentially hazardous situations in finishing, and as well as the issue of extraction of fumes and dust, there are also safety issues within your working environment, such as secure storage of harmful chemicals – out of the way of children and pets – and the correct disposal of waste. I am older and (slightly) wiser now, and this is my chance to alert all polishing newcomers to the potential problems inherent in the finishing craft.

Working environment

Let's start with the simple stuff. On the face of it there's not too much to be worried about when it comes to sharp objects here, but when stains are spilt or polishes are going wrong, panic is generally not too far away, and this is when you need to be especially careful while cutting rags or plastic sheeting with your Stanley knife (box cutter).

Another surprising hazard for the novice is wire wool. While the finer grades can be readily torn from the roll, the coarser types can easily cut you if you just grab some and pull. A pair of old scissors is a must for cutting coarse wool, and it leaves the roll looking tidier too. Also astonishing is the ease with which fine wire wool will catch light and burn. It may be hard to believe, but once it's going it is difficult to put out, and even if you stamp on it the slightest spark remaining will set it off again a few minutes later, so it's always best to get it outside and pour water on it.

A self-contained air shield system like this provides maximum protection from dust and fumes.

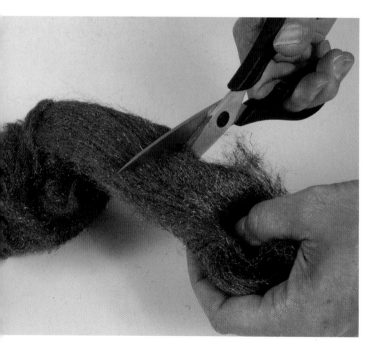

Always cut wire wool with scissors.

Wire wool loves to burn – only water puts it out.

40

Hasty wood repairs and last-minute cleaning up can also account for the occasional injury, as can an untidy workshop with cables and wires strewn around. It's all basic common sense really: careful planning, good working practice and a clean, organized working environment should help to keep you safe from harm. Make sure you have at least one first aid box or cabinet in your shop, and be sure you buy the type that doesn't need two hands to open. Do you know where your nearest Accident and Emergency clinic is? If not, make sure you find out.

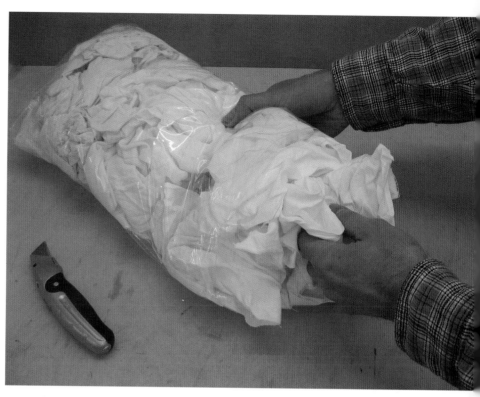

Be careful when cutting rags with your Stanley knife.

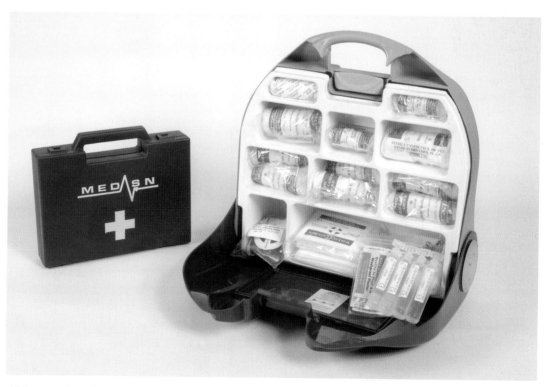

Make sure there is a first aid box close to hand in your workshop.

Dust

An ambient air filter is designed to run all day.

After spending years in the woodwork trade – years when health and safety concerns weren't considered overly important for the average employee – I shudder to think just how much dust of various kinds I must have ingested. These days health and safety is a top priority, and nearly all powered sanders are configured for easy dust extraction. As well as the health issues, efficient dust removal is a must for your finishing work, so consider investing in an ambient air filter as well as the direct type of vacuum extractor.

An ambient air filter will remove the tiny particles that remain, floating in the air, long after a job is finished. Next time you finish a sanding session, go back an hour later, preferably in the dark, and shine a torch into the workshop – you'll be amazed at how much dust is still there. This type of air filter is remarkably efficient and will run on as little power as that required by a light bulb.

Regularly check your extraction system for blockages.

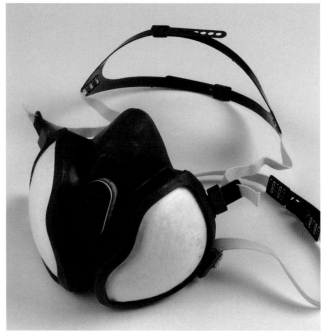

It's worth paying a bit more for a mask that actually works.

Poison

Finishing used to involve fairly harmless things like wax, turps, linseed oil and shellac and, while you might not feel too good, none of these would actually hospitalize you if you drank some by mistake. These days your average polisher is also dealing with a wide assortment of products fresh from the petrochemical industry, few of which have been created primarily for their 'harmless if consumed' characteristics.

To assist us in identifying the harmful and the deadly, all containers of hazardous substances on public sale must legally display a label identifying the contents, as well as safety information regarding usage, and action to take to avoid harmful contact. A manufacturer's telephone number is also required in case of emergency.

Heed the warnings.

KEY POINT

Despite taking all the precautions, if you do happen to find yourself feeling faint while working, don't try to ignore it – stop work and get out into the fresh air. It's unlikely your condition will do anything other than deteriorate if you don't.

Hazardous substances should be stored securely.

Fumes

You should look to avoid excessive exposure to harmful vapours at all times. It goes without saying that your workshop should be properly ventilated while finishing, and an extractor fan should be running whenever there are noxious chemicals being used. This might not always be possible though, so a good alternative is a closed air face shield system. These take the form of a full-face visor that is sealed around the face and has air pumped into it from a dedicated compressor. It really is vital you use one of these if you plan on doing any spraying, as the finely atomized mist of paint or lacquer will hang in the air for a considerable time – certainly longer than you can hold your breath for. Just make sure the air supply compressor is not in the same contaminated spray room environment as you.

Battery-powered face shields are a slightly easier way of achieving a similar degree of protection. These pump filtered air to the user's face within a sealed visor, and are popular with many woodworkers as they can keep both dust and fumes at bay and have no trailing lines to trip over.

Protective measures

Protect and survive.

It goes without saying that as much of the body as possible should be covered up when stripping or staining, so just reconsider your priorities on the hottest day of the year. While your skin will recover quite easily from all but the nastiest chemical burns, you never know what you might be allergic to so it's always best to be on the safe side, especially when using a new product. Eye protection should always be worn while stripping. It really is no joke to get caustic chemicals like stripper in your eye.

An eyewash station is good to have in the shop if there is no water tap nearby.

Safe handling

A common worry for most woodworkers and DIY finishers is how to dispose of the waste products that are inevitably produced during a finishing job. I'm sure most of us will have tipped the odd jar full of white spirits down the sink at one time or another without thinking. However, this isn't recommended, even for a big city with a sophisticated sewage system, let alone out of town, where it becomes more of a concern, especially if it's only a short run into a nearby stream or river and then finally the water table itself.

So instead of polluting your local environment, pour any waste products into a clearly labelled container and hand it in the next time you go down to your local tip. They will make sure it is dealt with properly, but just make sure it is stored somewhere safe and out of the way of pets and children in the meantime.

Help to keep your local streams and rivers clean.

Whenever possible, let your waste solvents sit on a shelf for a bit to allow the solids to settle out. The clear solvent left behind is nearly as good as new if carefully drained off, and anything else can be poured through a filter to remove most of the worst sediment. Just don't be too hasty when getting rid of waste, and generally try to be economical with materials wherever possible.

When storing waste products in containers they must be clearly labelled as hazardous. Dispose of correctly by handing in at your local tip.

Solvents can be re-used once the solids have settled.

Part 2
Finishes

2.1 Stains

I for one am glad that timber comes in a huge variety of tones and colours, but it's a shame that they're not all readily and cheaply available down at my local supplier. Until this is the case, or unless you have sufficient time, energy and funding to track down and purchase the exact wood species of your choice, it's likely that you may be considering a woodstain or two to lift your work out of the ordinary, or to match in with its new surroundings. Factor in the lack of choice at your local DIY store's timber department and the need for a touch of the exotic is more than understandable.

Timber comes in many colours . . .

Woodstains are an important part of the finisher's kit, and a fairly straightforward means of changing or enhancing the appearance of a piece of furniture. Fashions come and go with time: natural-looking timber will be popular one year, pale colour washes another and bold strong tones may be just around the corner (again). Stains and dyes can alter the look of a piece of furniture more drastically than anything else, so this is one skill you need to get to grips with before you go much further. With a bit of experience you'll soon learn which timbers suit which colours best, so feel free to experiment as you find out more about this fundamental art.

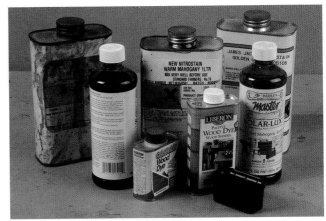

. . . as do timber stains.

(FOCUS ON:

Base basics

Stains are derived from many sources and are available for sale under many different names, but loosely speaking, can be divided into three groups: water-based, spirit-based and oil-based stains. It's at this point that I'd like to reinforce a very important point with regards to compatibility. I'm sure I can't have been the only one to brush on a finish to a newly stained piece of furniture, only to see the colour beneath start to come off before my eyes.

Why is this? Quite simply, the varnish or finish being applied has the same base as the stain, and starts to dissolve it before you know what's happening. To avoid this, it's vital to select a combination of stain and finish which won't react with each other in any way. For the novice this is something that should be taken seriously, although the professional can bend the rules a bit by deft application or use of sealer coats between incompatible products.

The earliest stains and dyes were obtained from nature.

Types of stains

Water-based stains

This is probably the oldest type of stain; throughout history people have been grinding up suitable compounds into fine powders, and steeping roots and berries in water, ever hopeful of a new colour or a longer-lasting effect. These days fewer amateur woodworkers are mixing up their own stains, but it still remains a viable and economical solution to anyone with a bit of time to experiment.

Older readers may be familiar with bichromate of potash and Vandyke crystals, both of which were widely used in the last century. These elements are obtainable in crystal form and are dissolved in hot water to whatever strength one desires. Vandyke crystals are naturally derived from walnuts, imparting a warm dark brown colour to your timber, while the potash is orange in colour, and darkens the timber through a chemical reaction. The fact that the solution created is extremely poisonous could possibly account for its decline in popularity in recent years. For me, the biggest drawback with water stains is the way the wood grain is raised in the process, leading to extra sanding work and the possible need for touching up the stain again afterwards. The biggest plus point has to be the low cost and the

Old-style crystal stain.

Water – safe and cheap.

range of bright 'paint box' colours available, and of course the scope it gives the enthusiast for experimentation. A painter friend of mine said he occasionally used beer (mostly stout) on staining jobs which produced very satisfactory results.

51

Spirit-based stains

A spirit stain is an alcohol-based solution with a coloured chemical compound fully dissolved in it. Generally ethanol is used as the alcohol – or 'spirit' – but readily available meths (denatured alcohol) remains an option for those wishing to make or dilute their own. Alcohol evaporates very quickly, which means that the stain has to be applied with considerable haste, making it unsuitable for the outright beginner or for a job with a large surface area to be covered. It has to be applied confidently and quickly to ensure a uniform coverage without visible lines, streaks and over-stain. However, a wide range of ready-mixed wood tones and shades are available so don't discount them entirely, but do try and restrict their use for smaller items and avoid large flat areas like table tops and floors.

Like water stains, spirit stains can also be purchased as powders. These give the woodworker even more scope for matching an existing timber, and for taking their finishing skills a further step forward. Stains can be mixed with meths/denatured alcohol from scratch, or powder can be added to French polish – also spirit-based – to make a coloured glaze.

Oil-based stains

Probably the best known and most popular of wood stains, an oil stain is generally my first choice for ease of application and dependable results. Based on a light oil like naphtha or white spirit, the colour pigment is held within by a chemical 'binder', but does tend to create slightly more of an opaque effect which can obscure the wood grain to a small degree. One coat is all that's needed as, not only will a further coat be unnecessary, but there is a risk that the second will partially dissolve the first, leading to a blotchy or patchy appearance.

Oil stains go on easily, and are forgiving to the amateur. Available in a large range of colours, I've found them quite amenable to both dilution with white spirit, and mixing with each other. Unless you've got a great memory or keep a fastidious record of all your stain experiments, make sure you mix up enough for the job in hand.

Oil stains do take a bit longer to dry however, and I like to leave at least half a day, or preferably overnight, before proceeding with the application of the finish.

Stain can transform an ordinary job.

Powders can be used to mix your own colours.

Aniline dyes

Aniline is an oily, liquid organic compound that is a by-product of coal tar processing. A mainstay of the dye industry since the mid-1800s, it is used as the starting base of many dyes and as an aid in the manufacture of lots of others. For this reason many dyes have the word aniline in their common name, such as aniline black (one of the best black dyes known), aniline red, yellow, blue, purple, orange, green and others. Today these synthetic dyes have largely replaced the natural ones derived from organic sources. In woodworking, the term is used generically to cover all soluble and transparent wood dyes, whether they are actually anilines or not.

Intense colours are achievable.

Powder colours

These are powdered pigments, available in a wide variety of colours and designed to dissolve in a particular solvent, be it water, spirit or oil. Useful to have, they can be used to make up a one-off dye or to tint a final coat of finish as a glaze. Make sure that all the powder is fully dissolved before use and strain it if necessary.

Home-made stains

In this category have to be included the emergency get-out-of-jail stains that are needed *right now* and have to be made from whatever comes to hand. As you're scrabbling through the cupboard under the sink looking for anything with a bit of colour in it, or scanning the shelves of the nearest 24-hour supermarket, trying to decide between gravy browning or shoe polish, you realize that 'stain' is an all-encompassing term and discover an increased respect for ancient peoples with their barks and berry juices. Yes, as long as it turns your wood the right colour, and doesn't react with the final polish, pretty much anything can be considered as a stain, but be sure to make a thorough test run first.

Ink is pricey for a big job, but ideal for an emergency cover-up.

Stains work really well on skin too, so always wear gloves.

Applying your stain

Always try and get it right first time.

A general rule of thumb when staining is to get it on quick, and to avoid going over the work more than once. Before you start, have a final check that the preparation has been completed, and that any holes have been filled and blemishes dealt with. By its very nature, staining is an operation with huge potential for spillage and spatter damage, so make sure you're somewhere where a spill won't be a complete disaster. It's worth pointing out here that a dropped container of stain can result in splashes that can travel an extraordinary distance – I know from experience this to be the case. A dust-free environment is a definite advantage and you will need efficient ventilation as well. Throw in good natural light, a comfortable temperature and you've got the perfect working conditions, and could probably rent out the premises to a professional polisher when you go away.

Planning

If you've got a big job in hand, try and break it down into component parts, removing doors and glass, hinges and fittings before you start. Make sure you plan your staining so that you can:

- complete separate areas before starting on the next
- if necessary, stain individual components before final assembly
- keep working wet edges to a minimum
- have someone on hand should you need to move a large work piece.

Start at the 'inside' of a job and work outwards. Watch where you put your spare hand to avoid leaving fingerprints, something that's usually only noticed when it's all dry and too late for an easy repair.

Stain can be simply applied with a pad.

Mutton cloth is extremely absorbent.

1 First stain any areas of contained moulding.

2 Follow up with the panel fields.

3 Finish off with rails and stiles.

4 This technique will result in uniform staining.

Technique

Generally a brush is used to apply the stain (with a rag standing by to deal with any runs) or a sponge brush, but I still prefer a piece of mutton cloth for my staining. This can be bought on the roll and is more absorbent than your average rag, meaning fewer trips back to the stain container for a refill. Whatever cloth or rag you do use, just make sure it's lint-free, as anything too fluffy will leave you full of regret and your work full of fluff. It's always worth having a brush on hand for any tricky areas that can only be accessed by a few bristles, and I like to use an old milk container to decant the stain into.

When working on a large flat area, like a table top for instance, apply your stain in long smooth strokes following the grain direction, and try to avoid breaking a 'line' in the middle. It's natural to start a stroke at one edge, but try to refrain from this as it's all too easy to cause a dribble or 'tear' down the side (fig 1). A method recommended by Charles Hayward, the notable and respected woodworker of old, is to start the stroke about 1in (25mm) in from the edge, and to finish the following stroke with an upward slant to cover this gap (fig 2). Repeat this process for the whole top, then remove all surplus stain with your mutton cloth.

An ad hoc stain container.

Fig 1

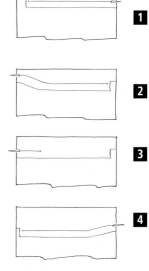

Fig 2

Stain absorption

If all timber was uniform and absorbed the stain at the same rate, things would be a lot simpler, but as it is, one or two precautions need to be taken to help avoid a blotchy appearance. The best thing you can do is to make sure you have a few off-cuts to hand that were left over from the construction itself. It's particularly useful if there is a good selection to choose from, including end grain, mouldings and some reasonably sized flat pieces. Obviously absorption is something that varies from timber to timber, and from job to job, so a little bit of experimentation at the start will pay dividends on your finished piece.

There are quite a few variables here, but broadly speaking, the better your preparations have been, the more consistent your staining will be. Where it's easy to come unstuck is in areas of wild grain (such as can be found around a knot for instance), and particularly on end grains and carvings. With care, it is possible to ensure that these problem spots receive only the bare minimum of stain, and that pools of stain don't stand in these areas for any length of time. A professional polisher will identify these areas at the start of a job and often give them a light coat of sealer. This can be a thinned-down varnish, sanding sealer or finishing oil, but whatever you use, test it first on your scrap timber, making sure you apply the next stage product to remove the possibility of an unwanted reaction.

As you may have gathered, there's more to staining than simply slobbering the stuff on with an old brush. Plan the job thoroughly in advance and prepare your woodwork to the best possible degree. Have all you need close to hand before starting and make as many test samples as possible. Good luck, and don't be scared to experiment – just make sure it's on something of little consequence and not your latest masterwork. Oh, and don't forget your gloves!

A pre-stain sealer should be considered for wild grain.

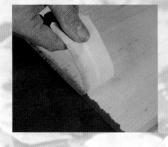

KEY POINT

Should more than one colour be desired on a piece of furniture, it is sometimes possible to mask off one area while applying stain to its neighbour, but success is far from guaranteed. Masking tape is fine for a relatively thick product like paint, but stains and dyes are much thinner liquids, and will often find their way beneath the tape despite your best efforts. The only way to ensure a clean break between areas of stain is to have them physically separate or to knife the border with a sharp Stanley blade. This is still a risky business however, and not one I would advise to the complete amateur.

Stains and dyes will always seep through.

TECHNIQUE:

Glazes

Sometimes the only way round dealing with a difficult wood – pine, maple, cherry and birch are the main culprits here – is to apply the colour after the finish. Yes, I know it sounds unlikely, but it is a solution nonetheless.

Prepare your piece to the normal standards required, dust off, then apply the first coat of your finish or one of a compatible sanding sealer. Allow to dry then lightly sand with a fine paper. The glaze is simply another coat of finish, but this time it is pre-coloured so as to achieve the desired result. Glazes can be made by adding concentrated powder colours or artists' oil paint to the finish. They can also be purchased from a decorator's merchants or a specialist finishing supplier, both of whom should have a good range.

As well as a straightforward colouring job, a glaze can be used to subtly tint the final appearance of a piece of work, or to suggest age and antiquity. Here the glaze is liberally painted onto the work, then wiped off with a clean cloth before it dries. This is the skilful part, and it is a matter of taste and preference as to how much glaze is left on. Sometimes it's sufficient to just fill the grain of the timber; other times you can produce the desired effect by leaving dark colour in the corners and mouldings to simulate the build-up of dirt over the years.

When dry, the glaze must be sealed in and here, once again, we are faced with the potential problem of the finish dissolving the colour beneath. If your next coat is, like the glaze, oil-based (i.e. it can be thinned with turps or white spirits as opposed to meths or water), then you run a real risk of undoing all your careful colouring. You should consider a water-based finish or, if you're happier with your oil-based one, then apply a light coat of shellac first to seal the glaze before the final finish is applied.

Liberally apply the glaze.

Moisten a rag with the glaze base.

Wipe off the glaze on selected areas.

Paints or powders can be used to tint the finish.

Apply the final coat of finish.

2.2 French polish

The aim of French polishing, which was developed by cabinet makers in France in the early 1800s, is to create the best possible effect with the minimum of materials. It results in a finish that appears to be part of the wood itself, and is considered by many to be the most flattering of all finishes to beautifully figured timbers and veneers. A French polish finish is not suited to every job, but it is the perfect choice for traditional, replica or any high-status heirloom piece you may have planned.

French polish production

Good light and a steady hand will get results.

Flakes of shellac.

Meths and ethanol. Note the marked difference in colours.

The main constituent part of French polish is shellac, which is made from the secretions of a tiny Indian bug called Laccifer lacca, and was originally harvested and imported primarily for the red dye contained in the raw material. At a certain stage in its six-month life cycle, the diminutive but valuable insect alights on a suitable host tree where it feeds on sap prior to secreting a cocoon for its eggs. Host trees include the kusum in India and the pigeon pea in Thailand, and many are cultivated for the express purpose of attracting the lac bugs. After hatching, the cocoons are shaken and scraped off the twigs and branches in the form of sticklac, the basic raw material. Sticklac production in India reached a height of 55,115 tons (50,000 metric tonnes) in the mid-1950s, slowly falling through decreased demand and increased competition from Thailand, to the present level of about 4,409 tons (4,000 metric tonnes). The next stage in the process is a simple washing in water to remove bits of twig and other large impurities, and the resulting resin is known as seed lac. Further processing includes melting and straining through hessian to produce button lac – the base of the familiar button polish – and stretching and crushing to produce flaked shellac. Finally, simple chemical treatments turn the basic shellac into a variety of colours – from bleached colourless through various golden tones to dark brown – and remove the small amount of naturally occurring wax. At this final stage the shellac is generally in flake form, and is now ready to be mixed with industrial alcohol, usually the clear denatured variety of which ethyl alcohol (ethanol) is the best known. Once dissolved in this way the polish has a shelf life of only a year or so, reason enough for many enthusiasts to mix their own to ensure known freshness.

The proportion of shellac to alcohol is sometimes referred to as the 'cut', and is generally 2–2½lbs per gallon, which equates to about 5oz (140g) of shellac flakes to 8floz (130ml) of alcohol. Ethanol, or its denatured equivalent (which has had a toxic substance added to it to make it unpalatable to all but the most hardened of alcoholics) is not always easy to find, but good polish manufacturers will supply it, sometimes under a different name. More readily available for the home polisher is methylated spirits. This is one step on from denatured ethanol and has had a violet-coloured dye mixed with it to further decrease its appeal to desperate drinkers. It can be quite a strong colour and is not welcomed by the polishing purists mixing their own finishes.

French polish today

French polish comes in different tones, from pale – or nearly clear – through white, golden, amber, red, button (mid-brown) and garnet (dark brown) to black. Most polishers have their own preferences, but I suspect few would be without a jar of button polish on their shelves. As in most fields, research and development continue apace, and there is now a tougher French polish available from specialist suppliers which is designed for table tops and is also easier to apply.

Whilst French polishing is still very much at the forefront of high-end, top quality hand-applied finishes, a new generation of furniture makers and designers are busy 'rediscovering' this venerable craft.

Shellac remains soft for 24 hours after application.

Ordinary furniture can be drastically improved by a French polish job.

Under the guise of re-interpretation, today's aspiring makers are trying to reinvent the difficult and time-consuming process that is French polishing, and to come up with an equivalent finish for the 21st century that is easier and quicker to achieve. To some extent they are succeeding, but a truly top-class French polishing job still retains its place as the acme of its craft.

Getting started

As befits the 'Rolls Royce' of finishes, the work it is applied to must be finished to the highest standards; anything less will soon be cruelly exposed as the rushed or skimped preparation that it is. Whereas many lacquers or varnishes will lay on the surface of the wood in a thickish film, partially obscuring what lies beneath, French polish seems to become part of the wood itself and will readily show up any scratches, flaws or filler.

Grain filling

Even more care should be taken than usual when a French polish finish is planned, and you should go down through the grits, and finish on at least a 320.

Some of the materials employed by the professional. Good results can, however, be achieved with less.

Depending on the nature of the timber, grain filling should be considered at this stage. Grain fillers can be bought at your local suppliers, and are available in a variety of tints or a neutral. Grain filler can be water- or alkyd-based, and it is a blend of filling and colouring pigments – usually an extremely fine silica – mixed to a heavy, thixotropic paste. This means it is thick in consistency but will flow like a liquid when compressed with a spatula or squeegee, essential so as to get into every open pore of the wood. It's possible to make your own, but I'd recommend purchasing it ready-made.

After application, the grain filler should be left briefly to dry, then the surplus is rubbed off with a piece of coarsely woven cloth, like sacking or similar. If permitted, the paste will fully dry, and removal of the surplus will be a much tougher job than planned. Regardless of base, all grain fillers are sufficiently neutral when dry to permit any type of finishing without fear of reaction. Rather than have an excess of fillers in stock, the professional finisher will generally stick to one neutral type and tint it themselves to match the work in hand, often with powder stains.

Once the grain filler is fully dry, use of fine wire wool or sandpaper will remove any last traces. Depending on the type of filler used, and whether or not it has been coloured, it's possible that the first coat of polish will pull some of the colour out, but this is not a big problem and further coats will not be affected. Some polishers like to seal the filler with an initial coat of button polish, but this should only be considered if the piece has been coloured very dark.

First coat

I expect most of us are familiar with the French polisher's rubber, the soft pad wrapped in fine cotton rag with which the polish is applied, but for most jobs, the first coat of polish is best applied with a mop brush. This is a very fine and soft-bristled brush, not dissimilar to a make-up powder brush, and is only available at specialist shops. Squirrel hair is the best in my opinion, but there are two or three other blends or varieties available, so there is something for everyone. Sadly they don't come cheap, but if you're

A mop brush is essential for achieving a consistent and effective first coat.

The luxury of choice – but it's good to have at least one mop brush.

serious about your finishing, or are just starting out in business, you won't regret the outlay as, properly looked after, a good mop brush will last for years. French polish dries very quickly, so it's best to leave your brush suspended in a covered jar of polish or meths when not in use. If it does dry out and go hard, don't panic and try to break all the polish out by crushing it in your hands – a few minutes soaking it in meths or alcohol will have it back to normal.

The first coat of polish can be thinned 25% with denatured alcohol or meths; apply this with the brush in a gentle 'laying on' method that is nothing like a rushed paint job on a garden gate. Follow the grain wherever possible, and avoid re-coating areas already covered. The brush allows awkward areas such as mouldings and carvings to be reached, something that's not always possible with a rubber. Polish dries quickly, so it will be ready for rubbing down in less than half an hour, depending on local climate conditions.

Polish takes hours to harden, so don't handle it unduly or it will 'print'.

Softly apply the polish with your mop.

Making a rubber

Despite its fine bristles, even a mop brush will leave brush marks behind, so the majority of polish coats are applied by rubber. A rubber is simply a pad composed of a soft clean white rag wrapped around an absorbent core of cotton waste or similar. Purpose-made wadding is available for this job, and the finished pad should resemble a pear shape, with the round bit held in the palm and the pointy tip by the forefinger. When squeezed in the hand or pressed against a piece of waste or test timber, the rubber should leave a mark of polish, but not so much as to be running drips.

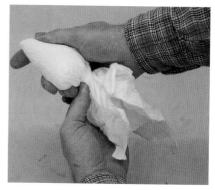

7 A twist will hold it all in place.

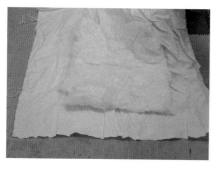

1 Take a square of clean rag and a piece of wadding.

4 Try and avoid it going loose or sloppy.

8 Unfold the rubber to charge it with polish.

2 Form the wadding into a pear shape.

5 Emphasize the point at one end.

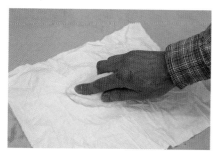

3 Fold the rag tightly around it.

6 Press the heel of the pad in firmly.

9 Test it out and you're ready to go.

Application

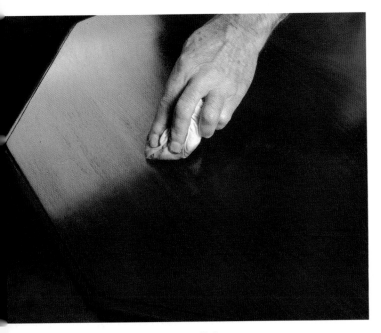

Keep the rubber moving at all times.

The polish is now ready to be applied. Make a series of light firm passes over the work, each one slightly overlapping the previous one, and both starting and finishing off the job. A gliding motion should be employed, and it is vital to keep the rubber moving at all times. Many polishers will advise the use of a circular or figure-of-eight pattern but, as with sandpapering across the grain, the patterns produced remain discernible until they are coated over by many further passes along the grain, so I tend to give them a miss myself.

Continue to apply polish until the rubber starts to stick. This is caused by the new polish starting to melt the earlier coats. When this happens it's a good idea to let the work stand for ten minutes or so while the polish hardens. Some polishers like to use a few drops of linseed oil flicked over the work at this point to lubricate the rubber and to enable them to get a bit more polish on in a shorter space of time.

In my experience this just further complicates an already difficult job and can easily lead to smears and trace lines which will then have to be painstakingly removed. At any point if the job seems to going wrong – and this can be anything from pulling off the earlier coats to a bloom developing – just stop work and let it dry. It's very tempting to ignore things and try to get some more polish on in an attempt to hide the problem, but you're better off rubbing back the affected area an hour or two later and starting it again from where you left off.

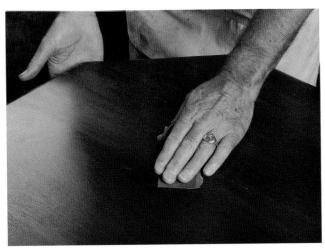

Rub down with very fine paper between coats.

Brush off any dust before starting the next coat.

Finishing off

After you've got a few coats on I find it's best to let the job dry for a bit, have a cup of tea, then lightly sand the work back with a very fine lubrasil or garnet paper, making sure to wipe off any dust with a tack cloth or a clean rag very slightly moistened with meths. While not in use, the rubber should be kept in an airtight jar or tin to prevent it drying out and going hard. Apply the next few coats and you will be starting to see a pleasingly good shine. Persevere until satisfied, stopping and sanding back as before.

The next step will really finish the job off nicely. Called 'spiriting off' it's essentially the same as before, but this time the polishing rubber is charged with a little meths or alcohol. Don't flood it, but merely show the meths bottle to the outer cloth of the rubber, then proceed as earlier. The alcohol will melt or dissolve the top layers of the polish, leaving the surface even smoother and shinier than before. Once happy with the job, leave it at least overnight to harden up – longer if you can – then wire and wax it with the finest wire wool and a good quality paste wax of a suitable colour. This removes any 'nibs' in the polish and softens the finish to a very nice warm shine. All you need to do now is stand back and admire, and just wait for those gasps of admiration from grateful and astonished family and friends.

An airtight jar is essential.

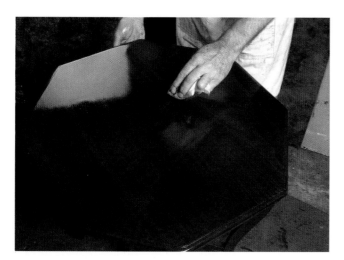

Spiriting-off is difficult but very rewarding.

A good finish is something to be proud of.

2.3 Wax

The smell of freshly waxed furniture wafting through the house at the end of a job takes a lot of beating and is often all that's needed to inspire a customer to put the kettle on. I make sure I always have some with me at the end of an installation on site or if I'm delivering a finished piece of furniture; it's the perfect way to add the finishing touch of the craftsman.

Most people seem to have a romantic impression of wax finishes, and associate the muted sheen, the pleasing touch and 'hand-finished' appearance with everything idyllic and 'olde worlde'. While there is much furniture around with a finish that possesses all of these enviable characteristics, it's usually been hard-earned and will often have been developed over many years, along with a rich colour and desirable patina. It is certainly admirable for anyone to try and emulate this effect, but the scope for disappointment is depressingly wide, and a casual application of a coat or two of a supermarket furniture wax just won't cut it.

Fortunately, there are ways to successfully achieve something approaching the desired effect, and a wide range of products available with which to help reach this goal.

Getting started

Appreciate those bees.

Wax has been in use as a finish for thousands of years, and beeswax is undoubtedly the most venerable of all waxes, remaining popular today as a constituent part of many of the proprietary wax products available. For a long time the only wax around, beeswax on its own is too hard to apply easily and must be softened by the addition of a solvent. Originally turpentine was used, but today solvents distilled from petroleum, such as mineral spirits and toluene, are widely employed. To the unsophisticated, all furniture waxes appear to be much the same, but everyone I know has their own likes and dislikes when it comes to choosing a finishing wax – often known as a paste wax – and it's not just the colour or the smell they're interested in. Depending on the proportions of the active ingredients, one wax can be markedly different to another. At its most basic, a polishing wax will consist simply of beeswax that has been melted down and blended with turpentine. This is a straightforward wax, preferred by many, but I like my polishing waxes with a little carnauba wax as well.

Carnuaba is a hard wax derived from the leaves of the Brazilian palm tree, and is too brittle to be used as a wax in its own right. Typically a good quality paste wax will contain up to 10% carnauba and, while it may make the wax a little 'stiffer', a deeper and richer sheen is obtained, and one that will last longer as well.

When to use wax

Wax as a finish on its own will nearly always prove to be less than satisfactory, both in appearance and for the protection it provides. If you were to apply wax directly to an unfinished surface, it would require many applications over a period of time before it started to produce anything like a shine, let alone a deep one. Even then the protection afforded would be close to insignificant, and out of all proportion to the effort used in applying it. Unfortunately, wax provides no significant protective barrier for wood against heat, water, chemical spills (such as alcoholic drinks) and so on. Because it has such a low melting point the first hot cup of coffee would melt straight through it and before long your table top would look more at home in a truck stop cafe.

Wax is probably best used as a final polish over an existing finish such as lacquer, varnish, shellac, polyurethane or even oil finishes, where it will give a little extra protection from light knocks and scrapes, as well as that softness of appearance that we all love. Wax is ideal for very low-wear items where the natural wood look is wanted, such as carvings and turnings, small boxes and exposed beams. There's no denying that a regular application of wax will keep all your furniture looking cared for, and can be especially useful in filling small scrapes and scratches. Coloured waxes can hide a multitude of blemishes.

Applying wax

As with many things in life, little and often will achieve better results than too much all in one go. The more wax that you try and get on in one application, the harder the buffing-up process will be; plus you run the risk of build-ups in tricky corners or mouldings. For furniture with an established finish, simply apply the wax polish of your choice with a soft cloth, in quantity somewhere between sparing and almost liberal. Leave the polish to dry – the time may vary according to type, but the supplied instructions should put you straight – then vigorously buff to a deep sheen with a soft cloth or pad.

Wax is best applied with a soft cloth.

Rub it in well along the grain.

Leave to dry, then buff up to a shine.

Wax is great for maintaining the looks of nearly all furniture.

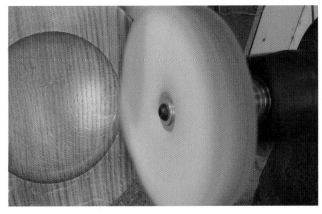

A mechanical buffer can make it easier for awkward shapes.

When dealing with a new finish, for example French polish, a coat of wax will help soften it down a little. If you feel the finish has come out slightly more glossy than expected, apply your wax with a pad of extra fine wire wool – either 000 or 0000 grade – which will have a gentle abrasive effect just sufficient to knock the edge off the shine. It goes without saying that this wax will also make your piece of furniture considerably nicer to the touch, something that is often underestimated by a surprising amount of woodworkers.

. . . creating a superb finish.

After a French polish comes wire and wax.

The fine wire wool slightly mutes the shine . . .

Briwax can transform a piece of furniture.

A purpose-designed 'wax off' brush fits on your power drill.

Wax types

Briwax

Briwax is unlike most other waxes currently available on the high street, and seems to perform in a slightly different way as well. It has a high toluene content – this is what the various waxes are dissolved in – which evaporates at a surprisingly fast rate. The work needs to be buffed up almost immediately, and very soon the wax appears to 'skin' over, settling down into a relatively hard finish. However, care must be taken when applying Briwax over an existing finish as it will remove oil finishes and soften lacquers if not buffed off quickly enough. Toluene is a poison and the fumes can be challenging during application, especially in a small room. This is another job where speed is of the essence, and you might find yourself in a bit of a waxing frenzy once you get going. Despite its shortcomings, Briwax does look good on pine, old and new, and has been used lovingly by many an antique furniture dealer over the years.

The standard neutral Briwax has a sort of an opaque effect on timber and, in my opinion, is partially responsible for the continuing popularity of stripped pine furniture and internal doors, making a good job of enhancing a piece for minimal outlay of money and effort. I wouldn't use it for a door myself though, because it marks very easily, especially from water splashes and so on.

Liquid wax

This is simply a paste wax which has gone a bit further in the diluting process, and doesn't really have too much to recommend it, as it contains only a small proportion of actual wax. However, its biggest asset has to be its liquid form and it is popular for carvings or anywhere else that could be prone to build-up or clogging. It can be simply applied with a cloth or dedicated soft wax brush.

Wax is the most versatile finish enhancer.

Wax sticks

Although not strictly a finishing wax, wax sticks nonetheless ably assist in the process. It has also lately become my first choice of furniture filler, as stick wax can be used on any pin or nail holes or similar blemishes after the finish has gone on and, carefully applied to selected areas, will blend in with polish, lacquer or varnish to produce an almost invisible repair. It's available in many wood tones, and can even be melted down and mixed to create your own custom wood shades. The wax must be gently heated and then, when soft, it can be combined, rather like modelling clay.

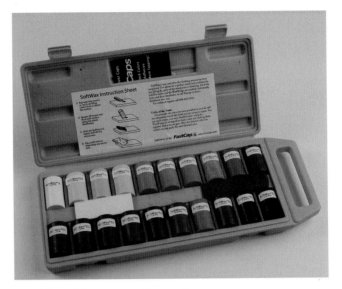

Wax filler sticks are great for repairs.

Black Bison

When I first started in antique furniture, the aroma of the polishing shop sometimes acted as a bit of a magnet and I often found it hard to leave. It took me years to find out, but a major part of the smell was this very brand of wax. It's an almost sweet smell, and not harsh like some of the turps-based waxes. Now you may think it would be ridiculous to buy a certain wax just because it smells good but, while I personally might be tempted, it's fortunate that the other characteristics of this superlative paste wax are equally special. Applied in the normal manner, Black Bison seems to manage to get a good shine regardless of any situation, although it could just be my rose-tinted glasses . . .

Black Bison wax – still going strong after many years.

Timber blanks are dipped in wax to prevent them from drying out unevenly.

Other uses

Barrier

As well as a finish, wax can also be an effective barrier against water vapour and general damp when applied in a thick coating to the end grain of boards or freshly cut wood. Because it is applied in such a thick coating, it prevents the moisture in the timber from escaping too quickly, thus ensuring that your boards dry out in a stable manner and are not so prone to shakes or other movement. You'll often see a coating on the small sections of exotic timbers sold as blanks for turners and carvers.

Lubricant

We all know that a solid block of paraffin wax or a piece of candle may be useful for easing a drawer or similar, but did you know that a thin coat of paste wax on the infeed table of your thicknesser is often just the thing to help persuade it to deal with those outsize boards of oak you've just acquired? There are purpose-made products on sale for just this sort of job, but in my experience, a wipe over with your waxy cloth will do just as well.

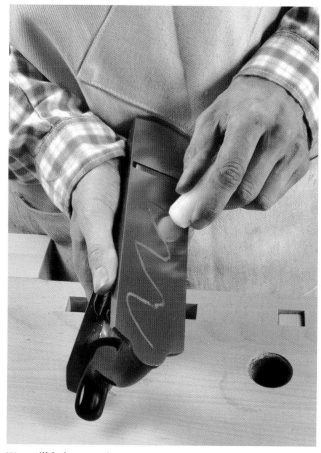

Wax will help on a plane . . .

. . . or a planer thicknesser.

2.4 Varnish

If there's one thing guaranteed to spark passionate argument, it's the use – or not – of varnish. Long associated with the bumbling amateur, varnish has through no fault of its own managed to acquire a reputation as a cheap and nasty finish. It is generally perceived as being a thick and uneven coating, complete with runs, curtains and bubbles throughout. Certainly we've all seen treacled finishes like these, and I think the manufacturers of coloured varnishes – whose adverts seem to imply that you should spend only the barest amount of time possible on a finish – have contributed to the devaluing of varnish as a pleasing protective finish for furniture and all things wood. A good varnish job, correctly applied and well looked after, will go on providing good service – that is, protecting the timber underneath – for many years to come.

Varnish through the ages

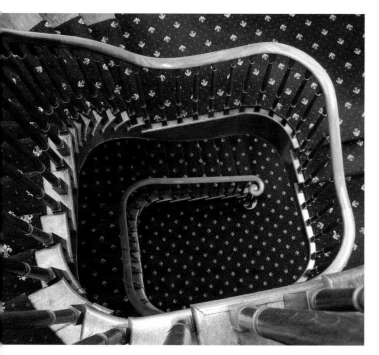

Varnish is ideal for areas of high wear.

The petro-chemical industry has been responsible for many advances in varnish technology.

Varnish is one of the oldest finishes around, and developed into what we know today as a result of the familiar human search for betterment and improvement in every aspect of the immediate environment. Naturally occurring resins were added to such plant and tree oils that were already in use as a protective finish, and were found to improve both protection and overall quality. Crude alcohols were also enlisted as vehicles for dissolved resins, but it wasn't until amber was added to a heated oil-and-alcohol combination that a really hard-wearing product was finally created.

Tree resin has long been the basic ingredient in varnish.

For our purposes we must consider the three basic types, again separated by difference of their bases: oil, spirit and acrylic varnishes. Oil varnishes have long been the most useful type, but with developing technology in the chemical industry, water-based or acrylic varnishes are increasing in popularity.

Modern varnishes; acrylic versus oil.

Oil varnishes

These are made from a drying oil, usually linseed oil, reinforced with a resin of some kind and diluted with a spirit such as turpentine or white spirit. As the varnish dries, a chemical change takes place. The oil content absorbs oxygen and becomes a tough and somewhat pliable solid. This physical change is also helped by the spirit evaporating or thickening, or polymerization taking place leading to an alteration of the atomic structure and consequent hardening of the film.

As a result, varnishes which have a greater proportion of oil to spirit become naturally more pliable and elastic, and are termed long oil varnishes. It goes without saying that the reverse, where there is more spirit, gives a harder film and is known as a short oil. To assist in the hardening process, and to speed drying, liquid metallic elements – known as driers – are introduced; the downside to this is the increased vulnerability to direct sunlight which will crack and flake the varnish in a matter of months. There are many different varieties of oil varnish – here are some of the most common.

Alkyd

Instead of a naturally occurring resin, alkyd varnishes are made with a synthetic resin – a type of polyester – that is combined with the other ingredients, alcohol, acid and oil. This polyester is probably the most commonly used resin in commercial varnishes today, and produces a product that is durable and flexible, has good resistance to abrasion and is resistant to discoloration. Despite being less expensive than the other varnishes, they are relatively slow drying and will usually take 24 hours to dry properly for re-coating. It has hard-wearing qualities which make it a suitable varnish for finishing floors.

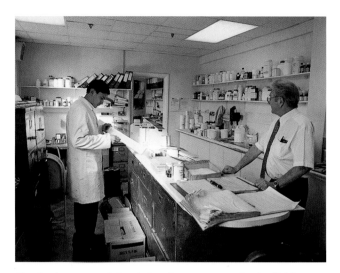

Continuing research has led to improvements in the field.

Polyurethane

This is essentially a modified alkyd varnish that has had polyurethane added to the mixture. As well as being very cheap to produce, polyurethane offers better protection against scratching than any other type of varnish. However, it does discolour quickly and is prone to cracking and flaking due to poor surface adhesion qualities. Being so commonplace and readily available, it is widely used for most varnishing applications.

Marine

For protection from the harsh conditions at sea, marine (or spar) varnishes were developed to provide ongoing and longer-lasting protection. In this varnish the oil content is increased – the actual oil itself is the superior tung variety (see chapter 2:5) – and the resin of choice is a blend of the aforementioned alkyd and phenolic types. These ingredients all combine to make an extremely durable and flexible varnish, but its high yellow colour and lengthy drying time mean that its use is primarily restricted to the marine environment it was intended for, although table and bar tops can both benefit from a few coats of this impervious finish.

Popular finishes

Spirit varnishes

These are little used by most professionals today, but with one notable exception – knotting. I expect we've all seen paintwork where knots and marks in the wood below have 'bled' through the layers of paint covering them. This is because the resinous secretions emanating from a knot will exert a solvent action on most paint types and make their way to the surface. Spirit varnish – or in this case, knotting – comprises shellac flakes dissolved in commercial alcohol, and dries by means of evaporation, leaving a continuous film of shellac which is impervious to the resin.

Spirit-based varnish, a.k.a. 'knotting'.

Acrylic varnishes

These are a relatively new type of finish, and tend to look less like conventional varnish than any of the other types. Often coloured milky white in the tin, and displaying a strange luminescence, some of these varnishes possess a curious, uneven consistency, leading the novice user to suspect it's 'gone off' or is past its sell-by date. Extremely fast drying, it is also virtually odourless, but its lack of body tint can leave timber looking a bit 'cold' or colourless. They are reasonably hard-wearing, but technology is improving all the time, so should only get better. Acrylic varnishes are not advisable for exterior work, but are just the job for the impatient furniture maker amongst us.

Shoddy preparation will always out, just like these knots.

Oil-based varnish is golden brown; acrylic is opaque white.

Success with varnish

If you're looking for a quick and instant result, then perhaps you need to re-evaluate your finishing needs. A good finish doesn't just happen by itself, so you can't expect to grab the nearest brush, open a tin of varnish and achieve perfection ten minutes later. This is where most varnishers have been going wrong, and is the sort of thing that has led to the battered reputation which has burdened this product over the years.

Preparation

I'm hoping you'll have read chapter 1:2 by now, and have prepared your piece to the highest level attainable with the equipment and materials you have at hand. Some consideration to the varnishing environment should also be given, and a dust-free room should be top of the list. Because most varnishes are comparatively slow driers, every freshly varnished surface – especially the flat ones – presents a trap for whatever is floating about in the air, and too much dust and other airborne debris can spoil an otherwise good finish. If space is at a premium, you may be tempted to work out of doors on a nice summer's day, but believe me, you'll soon regret it, as every bug and fly in the area will quickly be attracted to your freshly varnished workpiece.

Varnish is tough, durable and looks good.

Always be sure to rub down between coats.

KEY POINT

I think it is the similarity with paint that affects the way most people treat varnish; after all, it comes in similar tins, goes on the same way with a brush and usually takes overnight to dry. This way of thinking should end now, and the first thing you can do to reinforce it is to never shake a new tin of varnish in the same way as you might a new tin of paint. Doing this creates many tiny bubbles, all of which will need to be brushed out or else stay forever visible on your finished woodwork.

Stirring

Satin or matt finish varnishes should be gently stirred (a quick inspection of your stirrer will soon indicate if much more stirring is required), whereas a gloss

Varnish – stirred, not shaken.

varnish is ready to go from the shelf. This is because it contains none of the flattening paste (usually some kind of zinc oxide) that is used in satin and matt varnishes to prevent the light from reflecting off the surface and thus giving a duller, more muted shine. This paste generally sinks to the bottom with time, thus requiring a remix with the rest of the varnish before use. It can also have an obscuring effect on the grain of the wood beneath, so if you're planning a multi-coat job, then use gloss right up to the last coat or two and finish off with your satin. Failing that, use gloss for the entire job, then just give it a good going over with fine wire wool to kill the shine.

Some of the coloured varnishes require more in the way of stirring treatment, but I hope that no one who reads this book will ever use this type of product again and will stain their work instead, before applying a clear finish. As well as obscuring the grain and beauty of the wood, coloured varnish looks particularly bad as soon as it chips off and leaves the lighter timber underneath exposed for all to see.

ⒻFOCUS ON:

Tools

Like most jobs, having the right tools makes things much easier, so a good brush or two should be high up on your shopping list. Lighter-coloured bristles are generally finer than the darker variety, and this is just one more factor that will help towards giving you a better finish. The more of these seemingly insignificant details you attend to, the more your chances of success will be increased.

As well as getting the right-sized brush for the job, make sure you have a couple of other sizes standing by just in case. Although a smaller brush will be cheaper to buy, the extra time you take – and the finished results – will make it an expensive economy indeed, especially on

Buy the best brushes you can afford.

larger surfaces. I still have trouble parting with money for the 'best' or most suitable tool, but I know that if I don't I will regret it – if not on this job then on the next. With a top quality brush you get away from a 'disposable' mindset, and start thinking about looking after your investment, which can only be a good thing.

First coats

When my granddad used to thin down paints and varnishes we would think he was just being a cheapskate (and continuing the family tradition). I realize now that there are times when thinning is actually called for, and one such occasion would be before the first coat of varnish. If you plan to apply many coats, it's a good way of improving the bond and adhesion between the varnish and timber, as the thinned product is absorbed more easily by the grain.

With a slower-drying product, applying a sealer coat – varnish thinned 50/50 with white spirit (if you're using an oil-based varnish that is) – will also speed up the drying process sufficiently to allow two coats to be applied on the first day, along with a combination of good luck and optimum drying conditions. A thinned coat also goes on more easily, especially round difficult areas like carved or moulded details, and helps to avoid the finished job looking too 'sticky'.

The first coat is the thinnest.

Thinned varnish goes on nicely with a mop brush.

Brushing

Varnish should be applied in an unhurried manner – even the sealer coat. At the very least, make sure you finish up with an even coat all over. Always start from the 'inside' of a job, and work back towards you. The natural instinct is to varnish the nearest thing to hand – a mistake because this will be the bit you'll need to hold to move the work around.

After applying your varnish to the work surface, it's important to 'lay off' with the tips of the bristles in order to achieve a neater finish with minimum brush marks, and to avoid build-ups in corners and mouldings to prevent runs later on. Tops – and other large areas – will benefit from this treatment, and it is here that the importance of selecting the right-sized brush for the job becomes apparent.

If your workpiece is too large or it is not convenient to lay the work on its back or side, any other large areas will have to be varnished in the vertical position. While this isn't a huge problem, whenever gravity is involved there is always the danger of drips and runs. Brush the varnish on horizontally across the side (and across the grain too), and then lightly lay off vertically, immediately afterwards. Keep checking back for build-ups and potential problems all the time you are working.

Sanding down

When the job is fully dry, give the work a light sanding with a fine paper (something around 240 grit or slightly coarser as it is the first coat) before dusting off and applying the next coat. Take the same precautions against drips, runs and build-ups and you will see that this coat goes on differently as the timber no longer absorbs the varnish, having been sealed with the first coat.

A further rub down and dust off prepares the way for the third coat – extra care should be taken here unless you want to apply further coats. Three coats is about right for most jobs, and gives a much better finish than two thick ones. The varnish will take a day or two to fully harden, so treat the new finish carefully for the first few days – you don't want all that good work undone.

A clear oil-based varnish will add colour to the work.

FOCUS ON:

Maintenance

There's not too much you can do for a varnished finish, other than keep it clean and free from assault with sharp implements and scorching flames, but it is possible to 'touch in' any highly visible chips or scratches. Lightly sand the area in question, taking care not to go through any further or expose the original timber (if stained), and apply a small amount of the original – or matching – varnish with an artist's paintbrush. Repeat as necessary until your chipped area is filled, lightly sanding between coats using a flat cork block or similar.

Chipped varnish will always look unsightly.

If you're varnishing any furniture or woodwork that will be out of doors, you will need to consider an extra coat or two, as the elements are always unforgiving to any finish. Be prepared to rub the job down and re-varnish every year though, otherwise the finish will soon be cracked and peeling, leaving the exposed timber stained and unsightly. I'm not a big fan of varnished garden furniture, an oiled finish is generally preferable; or consider using a timber that you know will weather naturally with grace and good manners.

An external door will require regular maintenance to stay looking good.

Outdoor furniture is not a great candidate for varnish.

2:5 Oil

Oil finishes, as natural products easily derived from trees and plants, were applied originally with a view to timber preservation and waterproofing rather than any cosmetic sense. Early finishes included linseed oil, probably the most popular even back then, and any other readily available vegetable oil such as poppy-seed and walnut.

It's partly their penetrating qualities and also their relative ease of application that make oil finishes very popular today. Unlike varnish or lacquer finishes, which sit on the surface of the wood and appear to form a barrier between you and the timber, an oil finish will penetrate fully into the grain, producing an aesthetically pleasing appearance and protecting the wood at the same time. It's this natural look that goes a long way to explaining the popularity of an oiled finish for today's discerning maker, but this does mean that your surface preparation skills really have to be on top form.

Types of oil

Popular finishing oils; note the different colours.

Poppy seeds have long been a source of oil.

Derived from natural constituents, linseed and tung are probably the two most commonly available oils and, being examples of 'drying' oils, often form the base of many other proprietary 'oil' finishes currently on the market. A drying oil is one that will naturally dry and harden when exposed to the oxygen in air, unlike say, a mineral oil which needs the addition of chemical 'driers' for it to fully cure.

Linseed oil

As well as providing the raw material for linen, the flax plant gives up its seeds for the production of linseed oil, which has been used for centuries. The unprocessed oil is amber yellow in colour and in its original state is known as raw linseed oil. It takes some days to dry when left out in the air.

Many years ago the furniture maker would produce a special deep lustre oil finish by daily application of linseed oil rubbed in just by hand, generally for weeks, sometimes even for months. Some say that the best finish requires this hand finish to be repeated once a day for a week, then once a week for a month, followed by once a month for a year, then once a year forever, making it the finish that never ends, but continues to improve with age. Because of this extended drying time raw linseed oil is not overly

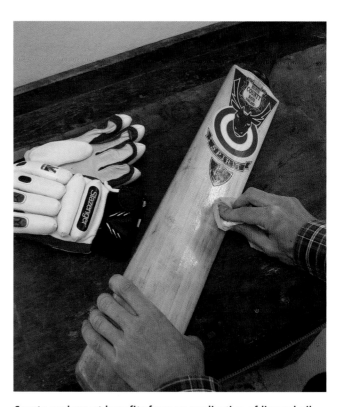

Sports equipment benefits from an application of linseed oil.

popular as a furniture finish, but remains the treatment of choice for cricket aficionados and gardeners, who find its penetrating qualities just right for maintaining a favourite bat or wooden-handled spade or fork. It's also pretty good for filling and weighting a new mallet.

Linseed oil, like linen, is derived from the flax plant.

It was soon discovered that if raw linseed oil was heated up, the drying – or cure – time was drastically reduced, hence the popularity now of boiled linseed oil. This often has oil-soluble driers added to it to speed the drying further, and provides a reasonable degree of protection for timber, but surprisingly little in the way of waterproofing – all linseed oils are equally inferior in this department.

The other type of linseed oil widely available is the refined variety, which takes the boiled version a step or two further. As the name suggests, the oil undergoes additional treatment, usually involving distillation, leaving a final product that is thinner and contains fewer impurities. Its use is primarily as an artists' medium, helping to mix and thin oil paints, and not surprisingly the extra cost of processing generally rules it out as a finish for furniture.

These days the use of linseed oil as a finish is restricted to restoration and maintenance of period furniture that has already been finished this way. But if you're a bit of a stickler for authenticity, then you might like to have a go at this most demanding of finishes – I just hope you're the patient type!

Oil is easily applied by rag or soft cloth.

Linseed oil can also be used to preserve and weight a new mallet.

Oils are a favoured finish for decking.

Tung oil-based recipes are very popular today.

Deck oils

Most of the finish manufacturers that I know of have made sure that they have at least one product in their range specifically designed for out-of-doors use, such as on decks and furniture. Most will be tung-based, but will always have other ingredients added to provide greater protection both to the elements and to ultraviolet light. There are so many different makes that I can't begin to recommend one, but in my experience most of them will need freshening up a bit after each winter. However, this need be no more than a quick rub down and the application of another coat.

Tung oil

Produced from the crushed nuts of the tung tree, tung oil originates from China and is another type of drying oil. It is similar to linseed but differs in one very important area: as well as being tough and flexible, it's also waterproof, making it suitable for many more applications. It is available in its pure or raw form, and also as a 'polymerized' variety – in this case, another term for heated. This treatment speeds its drying times and results in a slightly more glossy finish than the pure form, which has a matt appearance when dry.

Processed tung oils are usually applied in a wipe-on, wipe-off method with a short drying time in between. After the wipe-off and the coat has dried

Pure tung oil is thick and yellow.

completely, 0000 steel wool is used to remove surface irregularities, and the process is repeated. Depending on the look you're trying to achieve, you'll need to apply anything from three to six coats in this way. Tung oil is considered by many to be more durable than lacquer and is impervious to staining by water. What's particularly good about it is that minor scratches can be easily repaired by simply adding another coat, whether it be days or months after the last one. Pure tung oil is recommended for kitchen tables, chopping boards and similar food-related uses. Its non-toxic nature also makes it particularly appropriate for children's toys and furniture.

Tung oil can be used on stone as well as timber and protects each substance to the same degree. In recognition of its all-round qualities, tung oil forms the basis of many proprietary oil finishes and is the main constituent of teak, Danish and other so-called Scandinavian oils, which are generally a blend of tung and varnish with a little clear thinner. A recent newcomer is Organoil from Australia, which is a highly scented blend of tung, other plant oils and highly refined white beeswax.

Wiping oil

Wiping oil originates from the US, and although it is a fairly new product to most UK woodworkers, it could be argued that the various Scandinavian oils fit into this category. This composite product is based on tung oil, and also comes with one or two additives to make it easier to apply, dry more quickly and give more of a shine. Danish oil is probably the best known, but none I know have the thick consistency of American wiping oils. These are usually encountered in gel form – in reality, a consistency a bit like thin honey – and are just as easy to apply as a regular oil, with a soft lint-free cloth or rag.

Pure oil finishes are fairly easy to apply and generally enhance a piece of work, but do not offer much protection. You have to follow the 'lifetime' method mentioned earlier to achieve a finish that will repel anything and stand up to all sorts of abuse, and most of us just don't have the patience to wait around for 25 years or so.

Aware of this, some manufacturers started adding a compatible varnish to linseed or tung oil (sometimes with a bit of thinning medium as well to make it easier to apply), and produced a finish that was easy to apply like an oil, soaked into the timber like an oil, but dried quicker and harder – like a varnish. Many woodworkers make up their own wiping oil with a mix of one part linseed oil, one part varnish (oil-based, not acrylic), and one part turpentine. It's more than likely that, unless you're buying pure linseed or tung oil, then some varnish and probably other ingredients will have been added to the product in the tin. This isn't a big disaster, but until you know exactly what you've got, it's a case of finding the one that works best for you, bearing in mind that different timbers have different rates of absorption and may need a slightly thinner or thicker oil to look their best and be afforded the maximum degree of protection.

A wiping oil combines oil and varnish to create an easy-to-apply finish.

Applying an oil finish

For most woodworkers, this is often the best part of a job. Most of the hard work is done, and all that remains is to wipe on the finish to achieve instant, almost magical results. If you've got a nice bit of hardwood with a lovely figure, the moment you apply the oil the beauty of the grain just seems to jump out at you.

Prepare your work to the usual high standard. It should be dust-free and conveniently situated in good light, preferably with all-round access. Any staining should be carried out at least 24 hours before, using a water-based stain only.

Apply the first coat generously with a piece of lint-free rag or a clean brush, preferably one that has never been used for painting. I like to use a pale-bristled brush for oils and varnish, but you do need to be extra vigilant in spotting rogue loose bristles, especially on the top or more visible areas of your piece of furniture. Allow the oil to soak in for 10–15 minutes, then wipe off the surplus with a fresh piece of rag.

An oiled finish is suitable for most furniture.

Oil is very simple to apply.

Check again after half an hour or so for any seeping or runs you may have missed earlier. Leave to dry overnight, as an absolute minimum, and longer if possible. Lightly rub down with a fine paper, such as a 240–300 grade. I like to use lubrasil for this stage:

(FOCUS ON:

Oil safety

When an oil dries in the air, oxygen is released into the immediate atmosphere. This is called oxidization and is usually accompanied by an increase in temperature as well. If rags used for applying an oiled finish are screwed up and tossed carelessly in the bin, there is a very real danger of self-combustion, usually long after you have left the workshop.

It doesn't bear thinking about what this would mean for your tools, machines and timber, let alone any adjoining properties – and their inhabitants – to the workshop, so all oily rags should be carefully spread out or hung up to dry, preferably outdoors if possible.

Apart from this slightly disturbing characteristic of finishing oils, they're relatively harmless – the only other danger you might face is tripping over the open tin and slipping onto your back in a Chaplin-esque manner.

The right way to dry an oily rag.

And the wrong way.

as the name suggests, it is impregnated with a compatible stearate-based lubricant which makes the job easier, as well as giving a better finish.

Repeat the process for the next couple of coats. Apply at least three coats – more if possible. For the final sanding before the last coat goes on, use the finest paper you have, and an old piece at that. A new sheet can scratch your work with a sharp crease whereas a worn piece of sandpaper becomes soft and almost cloth-like to touch. Some finishers like to apply the last coat with the sandpaper itself as the dust created mixes with the oil to form a slurry-like filler which helps fill the grain and seal the pores of the timber, resulting in a deeper shine.

(KEY POINT

Choice of finish

After you've successfully applied an oil finish or two, this is one area where you can safely experiment. Different oils, as well as different oil blends, can give subtly different results, as well as providing varied degrees of protection. If it's a warm golden colour you'd like to bring out in a piece then linseed could be worth considering – this oil enhances a light timber such as maple or ash, as well as darkening slightly with age. Other oils are paler and won't lend much colour to a job, but this could make them better suited for birch or other very pale woods.

2.6 Spray finishes

There's something about a really well-applied spray finish that gives a job that genuine professional look, and once you've learned how to do it can be very satisfying indeed. The basic principle, which has been around for years, is nothing much more than air passing through a horizontal pipe and creating a vacuum as it passes over an adjoining vertical pipe, causing liquid to be drawn up from a reservoir and sprayed out in a fine mist. Technology has fortunately advanced over the years and the simple breath-powered spray diffuser has been supplanted by precision sprayguns with variable spray rates and adjustable fan patterns.

Safety

The biggest drawback to setting up a spray-shop, even a temporary one, has to be the clouds of airborne lacquer or paint which are an inevitable by-product of the technique. Lacquers have traditionally been cellulose-based and, despite their organic origins, have made the whole process a fairly toxic one, both for the operator and for anyone downwind of the fan extractor outlet. It's only recently, with the development of water-based acrylic lacquers and finishes, that it's become feasible to consider the occasional spray job at home, but unless you have very understanding neighbours or live on a farm or somewhere similarly isolated, it's certain you won't be allowed to make a regular thing of it.

Protection

More than any other finishing method, spraying exposes the user to considerably more danger and potential harm than they are likely to face elsewhere. Before any spraying is even considered, a full-face air-fed enclosed visor is a definite must, and a paper mask should at least be worn when rubbing down between coats. With so many toxic and potentially combustible and explosive chemicals involved, steps should be taken to ensure your spray room is suitably equipped to deal with any leakage or fire situation. UK (and US) legislation demands that all solvents and chemicals be fully labelled, listed and stored in a secure metal cabinet, further underlying the serious nature of this activity.

Spraying requires a lot of protection.

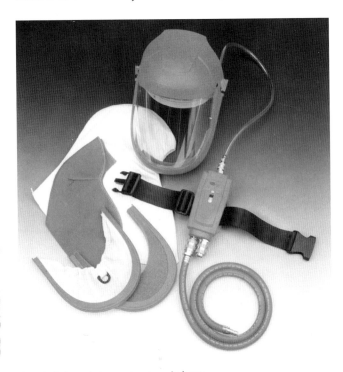

An air-fed containment set-up is best.

Extraction

One of the most important aspects is extraction. Not only is it no fun to work in a fast-growing cloud of airborne poison, it takes no time at all for visibility to drop and, even if you have managed to get a couple of coats on your work, it will be surely ruined anyway. This is because the tiny vapour droplets dry very quickly in the air and soon settle back down on everything in the spray-shop – including your freshly lacquered masterpiece – as a grey-coloured dust.

An industrial-quality extractor fan is the basic requirement here, preferably operating through a pair of wall-sized filters to prevent too much over-spray from being sucked out into the atmosphere. These will slowly clog up and will have to be changed regularly every few months or so, depending on usage. A correctly set up extractor will create a steady and powerful through-draught, immediately taking the over-spray out of the work area and in some situations will obviate the need for a separate full-face enclosed visor system to be worn. An air-fed visor like this will always be my preferred choice of protection though, and once you've acquired one you

A large extractor fan and a few thin boards create a knock-down spray booth.

might as well use it every time you're spraying, despite the slight loss of vision that sometimes occurs when the visor mists over.

KEY POINT

Water will always collect in the tank of a compressor, regardless of size, because the act of compressing the air causes it to heat up and then condense on the cold walls of the tank. If you use a pneumatic nail-gun or any other sort of air tool, you should always drain off the compressor after use – even if it's only been run for a short length of time – because any water present will travel down the hose or pipe and interfere with your kit.

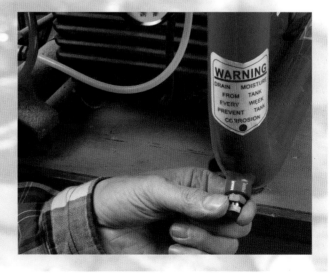

Professional set-up

A professional spray-shop will be fitted with a powerful compressor and a large-capacity tank to store the compressed air, connected by dedicated pipe-work to the spray room or booth itself. The compressor should be sited somewhere as far removed as possible from the actual spraying; somewhere that is obviously well ventilated itself. The airline is filtered to remove any traces of oil or dirt, and especially water, from the air.

Water is the nemesis of every sprayer, and will react with nearly all types of lacquer and paint to create a pale white blooming effect which will ruin the job. The bloom is the water vapour trapped in the finish and the affected area must be rubbed down or partially stripped to remove it. There are some days, especially in summer, when the relative atmospheric humidity is so high that it makes all but the most basic spraying impossible; indeed, a professional sprayer will prefer the winter months, as colder air will naturally hold much less moisture than warmer air can. All water must therefore be removed from the compressed air, and is usually taken care of by in-line filters, which can be doubled or tripled up according to requirements. A regulator – or pressure controller – is generally installed at this stage, and the sprayer will set the final pressure to be delivered to the gun according to what is being sprayed.

A compressor with a large tank is recommended.

Sprayguns

For most occasional or hobbyist sprayers, the standard spraygun (like the one pictured below) is more than adequate, but the difference in price and quality between a DIY gun and a professional one, such as a DeVilbiss, can be astonishing. Having used both I would not hesitate to recommend the professional spraygun every time and, if well looked after, it will continue to give top results for years, not to mention being easier to use.

Unless you plan to be spraying 24 hours a day, a gun like this will easily meet your needs, but most pros find it more convenient to use a bulk spraying unit. Here the finish is stored in a large tank or 'pot' and is connected to the gun by a further hose, making the gun lighter and easier to handle. Most importantly, it permits any awkward, upside-down work to be carried out, without fear of a vacuum block and the

resultant spattering as the paint or lacquer comes back in. These units don't come cheap, but if you've just had a lottery win you might well fancy one.

In-line filtering is essential.

A pot-supplied gun is easier to handle.

HVLP

This stands for High Volume Low Pressure, and describes a method of spraying that can be carried out with much less equipment. Typically a HVLP system will be based on a compact unit which runs continuously at low pressure and does not employ a storage tank for the compressed air. Utilizing a motor similar to that found on many dust-extraction machines, the air produced diffuses the product in much the same way as a high pressure set-up.

Aimed squarely at the hobbyist, reasonable results can be achieved with this type of system, although by its low-budget nature it is intended for occasional use only. Unfortunately this makes it likely that few, if any, of the precautions already mentioned will be taken by the user who just wants to blast a quick coat of paint on a door, for instance, and won't want to bother with extraction and full-face visors. It must be stressed however, that all spraying activities – even a two-minute job with an aerosol can – carry the same risks to your health and immediate environment, and every precaution must be carried out first.

Outdoors is best for small jobs, providing there is no wind!

A basic HVLP set-up.

Products

Finishes designed to be applied by spraygun have been designed and manufactured for just that job, and have a chemical make-up which permits them to vaporize efficiently and to dry extremely quickly to avoid runs and sags on vertical surfaces. Many of today's finishing products require little if no thinning to spray, and can be used straight from the tin. It may come as a pre-catalyzed product (i.e. the catalyst is added at the production stage and is activated on exposure to air), or a two-pack one where a chemical hardener must be added to make the finish 'go off'. I would recommend the pre-catalyzed paints and lacquers to start with, as these are easier to spray and the finish is suitable for all but the toughest environments. A two-part paint or lacquer applied by spraygun is one of the most robust finishes that can be achieved by the amateur, but is only really needed for worktop counters, restaurant tables and so on.

Many amateurs or newcomers to spraying may well make the mistake of trying to spray a standard domestic oil- or water-based paint or varnish with their new spraygun. It can seem like a good idea, as these are readily available on the day, or may be the exact colour required. However, these finishes are not designed for spraying and, as well as requiring careful thinning to the right consistency, will almost certainly prove to be a huge disappointment as anything but the thinnest coat, on anything less than a horizontal surface, will result in plenty of runs. It is far better to make the effort to track down the correct cellulose-based product from a specialist supplier.

Like many finishes of a particular base, cellulose lacquers are incompatible with other base products, and the maker's recommendations must be strictly followed. Use only the correct thinners at all times.

Working methods

There are one or two other things to consider when spraying, most notably gun set-up and air pressure. Depending on the product being used, a working pressure of anything between 35 and 70 pounds per square inch (psi) can be employed, but it's only experience, or trial and error that will inform you as to what you need. The spray leaves the gun's nozzle in what is known as a 'fan', the pattern or shape of which can be modified by simple adjustment on the gun itself, as can the rate of flow of product. Like the majority of sprayers, I prefer the vertical fan for most work, but there are occasions when the fan needs to be rotated 90° or reduced to a circular jet, depending on access to a complicated piece of work.

Technique

When starting out, it is vital to understand that the finish must be slowly built up coat by coat, and cannot be achieved in one sudden thick blast. Spray finishes are designed to start drying the second they leave the gun, and if correctly applied will remain where they are. However, spray on too much in one go and gravity will take over, resulting in unsightly runs, swags or curtains across your work. Scraping these off when dry, sanding back and doing it all

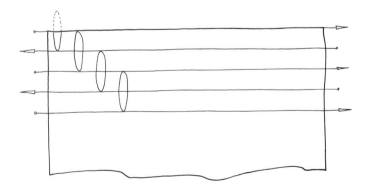

Maintain a fixed distance from the work and overlap each previous pass.

again is definitely not the way to proceed, so just don't be in too much of a hurry when you start out. Take time and practise to ensure you develop a steady technique which will apply the finish in a uniform manner, taking care to keep the gun a constant distance – about a foot or so – from the work. Make sure you start and finish by spraying off the workpiece – don't worry about the small amount of waste, it's far more important to get the job done right.

It definitely pays to exercise a certain amount of restraint and patience while spraying, and you will soon realize that applying more than one thin coat will quickly achieve the desired result. A light sanding must be carried out between each coat and, as most lacquers and spray paints are designed to dry extremely quickly, a successful finish can be easily completed in a very short time. A small batch of furniture can take just an hour or two to finish.

Useful aids

A small turntable is of considerable use to the operator in the booth; this enables the workpiece to be rotated so as to reduce the risk of touching the wet finish and to access all areas of the work in one session. Other useful props include adjustable racks or pegged timbers on which lengths of mouldings or beads can be laid. A board with nails protruding can be utilized to rest a freshly finished double-sided component on, and a similar board with suitably sized holes bored into it can be used to hold cupboard door knobs and other turnings of this nature.

Cleanliness

Regardless of which system you employ, cleanliness is possibly more important with spraying than with other finishes. Your gun must be scrupulously cleaned

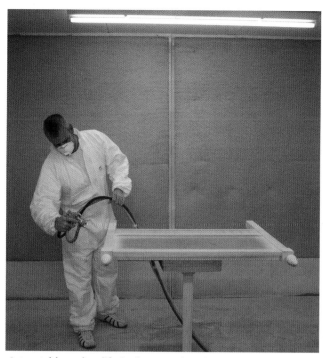

A turntable makes life in the spray booth considerably easier.

after use, both to ensure that the fine tolerance air-jets are kept clear and working and to prevent the chance of contamination from your last job to the next. Indeed, most professionals will have at least two guns, one for paint and one for clear lacquers to reduce the chance of even the smallest amount of paint ruining a lacquer job. Just remember to allow sufficient time and materials – rags, extra thinners or gun cleaner – at the end of a session to complete this essential task; you won't regret it the next time you're spraying.

Keep your spray equipment clean at all times.

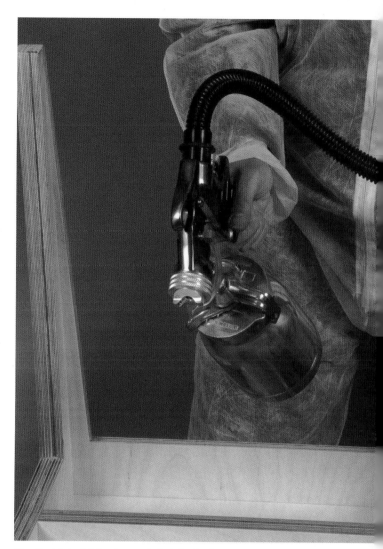

The 'inside' of this plywood chair is the best starting point.

I have to say, from personal experience, that the whole process of spraying can be extremely satisfying, but only if you have a suitable venue with all the requisite safety equipment in place. Of course, it will take a fair degree of practice and experience to be certain of a successful spray job, but the results can make it worthwhile every time. For most of us however, spraying is probably best left to the professionals, and if this type of finish is required, it's far easier to take the work to a suitable finishing company for them to do.

2.7 Floor finishes

By their very nature, finishes applied to floors have to be extremely hard-wearing, and conveniently quick to dry. This puts them into a different class of finish to your average polish or lacquer, and a purpose-made floor finish should always be used in preference to the regular kind. Most manufacturers have at least one such product in their range, although I would recommend a seal from one of the companies who specialize in this type of finish only. This is one area where development is constantly improving, so talk to a reliable trade source about how to get the best finish for your particular floor.

Traditionally, it was the constant maintenance (i.e. waxing and buffing) of a wooden floor combined with the friction effect of countless feet that helped develop any kind of shine. Today, no one wants to wait for a patina to develop naturally, me included, although you have to admit there is something special and pleasing about the gradual smoothing and wear that comes about naturally. As time pressures increase on construction and installation jobs, consumers demand that a floor is to be laid and finished as soon as humanly possible, if not before. This has led to the development of a new generation of acrylic finishes that dry quickly enough to allow two or three coats to be applied in one day.

Getting the floor ready

A badly prepared floor will stay looking that way.

A drum sander with edging sander; both widely available at hire shops.

From normal eye-level, most timber floors look good enough, but once you're on your knees looking for that diamond earring you've just dropped, you will soon see that this is not quite the case. Of course, some of us like to lay a floor to the same high standards as we would to any job, but more often than not the average wooden floor is given the bare minimum of the attention it actually deserves.

Nowhere is this more true than when it comes to preparation. Too often an enthusiastic amateur or casual professional will just go through the motions with the hired drum sander, neglecting the edges and corners and doing all they can to avoid fitting another expensive new sheet of abrasive. Factor in the time wasted driving to the hire shop and back, machine breakdowns, cord entanglements and 'deep ploughing' disasters and it's no surprise that many floors don't stand up to more than the briefest of appraising glances.

For most of us, having previously sanded no more than a table top, the enormity of the floor-sanding task soon becomes frighteningly apparent after the first couple of passes with one of these monster machines, and the temptation to just run away and leave it to someone else must be swiftly suppressed. Here then, are a few things to consider before, during and after the floor sanding process.

1 Can you afford to pay someone else to do it? It's a difficult, dirty, tiring and noisy job, and I've seen more than one floor ruined by inexpert sanding. Get a quote from a specialist firm or two, and ask to see some of their previous work.
2 If your budget won't stretch then you'll have to do it yourself, so plan things so that the house is empty for the day, and make provision to mask off the room itself and as much as possible elsewhere with temporary dust curtains. It's a cliché, but the dust really does get everywhere if you don't watch out.

Mask off internal doors.

Punch down any protruding nail heads.

3 Have a last check of your floor for any faults that may need attention and fill any knot holes or gaps at this stage. Punch down any protruding nail heads, something which is of particular importance when dealing with old floorboards.

4 Book your sanders (it's usual to hire an edge sander as well) in advance, preferably visiting the shop first to make it clear you want a decent one. Turn up early on the day to give yourself as much time as possible, and lay in a good stock of abrasive sheets or discs. You'll need more coarse ones than fine, and you generally only have to pay for what you use. Get some ear defenders too.

5 Unless you're strong, fit and able, you'll need a hand to carry a drum sander, so enlist the help of a willing friend.

6 Assemble your sander and fit the first abrasive sheet securely, you'll usually start with a 60 grit. Tilt the machine back, start it up and lower gently as you begin to walk forward. Don't let the sander dictate the pace – if you're not careful it will drag you through the wall.

7 For straight boards, work diagonally across the room in both directions, until the whole surface is flat, taking particular care to lift the drum as you near the end of each pass to avoid digging a trench along the skirting (if it has not been removed).

8 Once the floor is all flush, work your way down through the grades, following the direction of the boards – or the chevrons, if it is a herringbone parquet. This is likely to take some time, so be prepared for a hard day's work.

9 Keep a vacuum cleaner close by – it will make a big difference between sessions. Try to keep those bag-emptying breaks tidy and contained.

10 Work the edges and corners as best you can with the edge sander, or use your own orbital if you think it's up to the job. Hand tools may also be needed, such as planes or scrapers.

11 A lot of fitters don't bother with anything finer than an 80 grit to finish, but personally I think this is a bit slack – for a good finish you need to use a 100 grit at the very least. If you've got a good random orbital then you could run it over the floor at this stage – you won't regret it.

12 Finally, have a good clean-up and take the sander back to the shop before they close and you lose your deposit.

Floor stain

A warm, natural-coloured floor.

Hopefully you will have considered colours and finishes by now, and taken advantage of any scrap boards to make some samples. Just remember, darkening a whole floor can have a dramatic effect on a room. If you do decide to stain your floor, make sure you have all you need before you start and be prepared to work fast.

Many professionals use a mop-like pad on a stick for ease and comfort, but as long as your knees are still in good shape you will be fine with a brush and rag combination. My recommendation would be oil stains, but these need to dry overnight and you will still need to use a modicum of care to ensure a nice even finish. Work along the length of the boards, taking a group of the same number each time to avoid confusion. Don't stop halfway through; unlike a job I once saw where someone had stained half the room (and this was across the boards, not with them!), went on holiday and then came back to finish off a week later. Unfortunately, the resulting join line was visible forever.

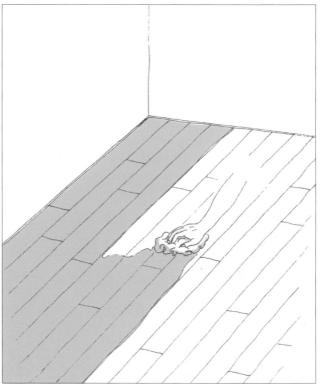

Divide the floor into regular sections to avoid confusion. Here, groups of four boards are being stained.

I can't emphasize enough the importance of preparing test samples, and if you've got sufficient timber to spare, make sure you stain or finish enough boards to give you a very good idea of how it will look. Some stains look harsh at first and need a day or two to settle down, particularly on softwood, so make your samples early on to get a true picture. Don't forget to apply several coats of your finish as this can affect the end result – another reason for making sure you have all your materials to hand before you start the job. As a general rule, the oil-based varnish type seals will give an amber – or slightly darker – tint to your floor while the water-based acrylic seals are virtually colourless. However, some older floorboards can sometimes react unexpectedly to any kind of treatment.

Applying the finish

Before applying the finish it's essential to remove all the dust from the floor, so make sure you have an efficient vacuum and take some extra time to dust off anything else in the room which might be a problem – including yourself and your clothes. If you can spare the time, it might be worth waiting overnight to allow all of the airborne dust to settle and then have another session with the vacuum cleaner the next morning before making a start.

Follow the manufacturer's instructions for preparation and application. Don't start thinking you know better, at least not until you've done it a few times and are sure of what you can get away with. Good ventilation is very important, but you also need to avoid having half your garden blown in through the open windows and settling on your wet varnish, so avoid starting a job on a windy day! Use the first coat to make sure you apply the finish in the most efficient way possible; at least if you paint yourself into a corner you can make good the damage before the next coat and know then to change your plan.

Try and work at a steady pace, and avoid pouring out more seal than you can deal with. You can work from a paint tray, but most pros I know just puddle the finish straight onto the floor and spread it around. An applicator pad on a long handle is a useful tool – not only does this speed things up, it also saves a bit more kneeling or crouching down, which is very welcome towards the end of a job. It's perfectly OK to use a large brush and, being closer to the work, this generally ensures a careful result. I have heard of a long-handled paint roller being used before, but I don't think the slightly textured finish it produces would be welcome on a timber floor.

Applying a finish with an applicator pad.

You will need to sand down the floor between coats, using a medium to fine paper to ensure a top quality finish. I usually do this by hand, although a simple ⅓ or ½ sheet orbital sander is OK, but keep it moving to avoid going right through the last coat. Follow this with another pass-over with the vacuum cleaner, paying special attention to the expansion gap around the edge of your floor or any other nooks and crannies where dust and fluff will collect. Two coats is the absolute bare minimum for a floor; three or four is my recommendation and anything more is a luxury bonus. Let's face it, when you consider the effort involved in completely emptying a room or two, not to mention all the dust precautions, this is not a job you want to repeat very often, so make sure you do it thoroughly in the first place.

Maintenance

Most modern acrylic finishes need little in the way of maintenance, just regular sweeping or vacuuming, with the occasional damp mop over it now and then.

A coat of wax a few times a year is a treat for any wooden floor, particularly if it's showing its age a bit, but be careful not to overdo it – it creates a very slippery surface and is even worse if your rugs and carpets don't have any grippers underneath.

If your floor is beginning to show signs of wear after a couple of years, clean the floor with an acrylic scouring pad and the minimum of water and detergent (don't flood it), or some wire wool and white spirits depending on the type of seal you will be using. Let it dry, then give it a quick going over with some fine to medium sandpaper, vacuum off and apply a couple of coats of varnish or seal.

A nicely finished floor is easy to keep clean.

A final cleaning with white spirit will help prepare a floor for re-coating.

If you leave it too long, the wear will go through the original finish to the wood itself, leading to a much trickier repair job, especially if there has been any staining involved.

Wax

If you want a really classy look, then you could consider a complete waxed finish, but this is definitely a high-maintenance expensive option. Some people start with the wax right away, but I recommend a couple of coats of an oil- or spirit-based sanding sealer first. Just make sure you have an electric buffer or polishing machine near to hand, or you'll be fit for nothing else all week. A wax finish looks good, but you will need a weekly re-application of something like Traffic Wax, or a similar liquid polish, to keep it looking that way. I decided on this finish for the ballroom in my Scottish castle and, I have to say, it's a much easier job with the help of a servant or two.

Oil

I remember being shocked some years back, when I returned to a job where I had recently laid an oak floor, leaving the finish to the customer as requested. I tried to hide my disappointment at his efforts, but I felt the floor had been ruined by the application of linseed oil. True, it had brought out all the figure in the 'rustic' grain, but the overall effect was drab and dull, and every mark and dusty footprint was clear to see. Unless you're a fan of the natural, muddy look, I would implore you not to consider this option at all. Like most jobs, careful planning and consideration of all factors – particularly desired appearance, available light, timber type and your budget – will pay dividends with a floor. Thorough preparation and diligent execution will ensure that the job will be one that you are proud of and which will last for many years.

Properly finished, a timber floor will look good for years.

2.8 Paint

Paint, I love it. In my early days, when most of the things I made were constructed from a variety of waste timber, scraps and off-cuts, a couple of coats of paint made the difference between a piebald 'harlequin' table and a sleek piece of contemporary furniture. There's a lot to be said for a coat of paint, and I bet I'm not the only one who's ever wanted to hide some less than perfect joinery beneath the camouflage of a drop or two.

You've only got to look at some of the items that are pulled dripping from the caustic soda tank at your local strippers to see why they were painted in the first place. Huge unsightly knots, areas of plaster filler and ugly grain colours lie hidden beneath smooth coats of white eggshell or gloss, and I say let them stay there. Paint is not really the villain it's often made out to be by furniture and cabinet makers – not all of us have the budget to work with expensive timbers and veneers, and a well applied paint job can look just as stunning when used on the right piece.

Getting started

A painted finish can look good even when worn.

A thorough and disciplined approach to painting will definitely pay dividends, and just because a paint job is often seen as inferior to the trickier furniture finishes doesn't mean it should be undertaken in anything less than a professional manner. Follow the same steps for preparation and execution and it will be just as rewarding.

Colour

What do I know about colours? No more than anyone else with functioning eyesight. There's a lot of theory written on colours, much of it referring to the classic colour wheel (see below). I think it all comes down to personal taste, so if you like it and most of your friends or family do too, then that's OK with me. Just make sure that you pick the right one first time as it's extremely tedious to have to start it all again if you change your mind afterwards.

Reach for the paint tin.

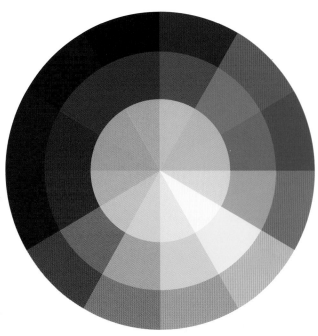

There is a colour here for everyone.

Brushes

You won't get far in painting without a brush or two, and it's important to choose them wisely. By all means buy one or two cheap ones from your local DIY suppliers, but you and your work will definitely benefit from a few good quality brushes in your kit as well. A good brush can either be natural animal hair or entirely synthetic. As with most things these days, production and manufacturing methods have greatly improved, and there is a large choice of top quality brushes out there. When choosing, make sure the bristles are even and plentiful and of a generous length, and that the handle is comfortable to hold.

Once you've used a top quality brush you won't be keen to go back to the cheap ones so it's worth making a direct comparison on a job to see how they both perform. Once you've invested in some decent brushes you will need to look after them, so if your usual method is 'use it then bin it', you might have to readjust your philosophy or resign yourself to poor results for ever.

Keep your brushes clean and dry, preferably loosely wrapped or in the now popular cardboard jacket that many come supplied with. Before use, dip your brush

Top quality brushes should be obtained.

in the base liquid of the intended paint, i.e. water for acrylics and white spirit for oil-based paints. Once shaken out, the brush is ready for action and not only will it perform better from the start, it will also be a lot easier to clean up afterwards. Try to avoid letting your brushes stand in a jar full of solvent 'between jobs', which is a sure-fire road to neglect and will result in some tough cleaning at the start of your next painting session. It is far better to clean as you go.

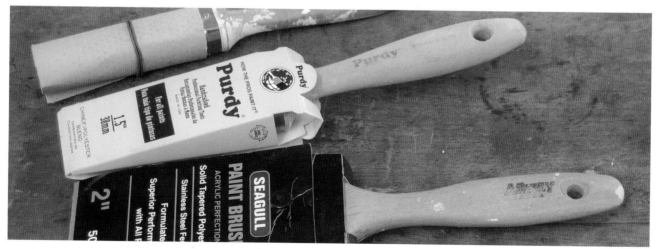

Brush care should not be overlooked.

Keep your kit together at all times.

A dedicated stirrer should always be available.

A proper can opener is a definite asset.

Sundries

A clean rag is always useful to have around when painting – not to mention dust-sheets to protect floors, both indoors and out – and I've recently found that products like disposable Painter's Wipes are an improvement on that. Impregnated with a kind of cleaning fluid, and also slightly abrasive, they will clean up stray splashes with considerable ease. You will also need empty jars, containers and turps or white spirit, as well as an old chisel or similarly blunt-bladed tool, and a clean stick or two for stirring. Possibly one of the most under-rated tools is the paint-can opener; no more frustration with damaging screwdrivers when you've got one of these in your kit.

Always be sure to work to a methodical plan.

A primer should be used on all new timber.

Pink primer is more visible on white paint.

Surface preparation

We've talked about woodwork preparation already (see chapter 1:2) and pretty much the same goes for preparing for painting too. With the exception of rubbing down old domestic paintwork like doors and skirting boards, I try to prepare everything I make to the same standards. It's a mistake to think that you don't need to prepare your work to a professional degree just because you're applying coats of thick paint rather than thin polish. If you're not careful you'll soon start letting your standards slip and all of your work will ultimately suffer.

However, it is true that a paint finish is more forgiving when it comes to preparation, and enables a variety of fillers to be used, none of which need to be particularly well disguised. It's possible that your constructional techniques can be a bit more agricultural too. You can make generous use of nails, pins and screws, and make any last-minute modifications that would normally be embarrassing to perceive through a polished or varnished finish. Just make sure that you use epoxy resin filler – like the two-part stuff used mainly in car body shops – for recessed screw-heads and other larger areas, because water-based fillers, such as Polyfilla, will shrink and crack over time, making the repair visible through the paint.

Dust

One thing's for sure: when it comes to dust, it's no more welcome on a paint finish than on any other. It's sadly inevitable that a fair amount of dust will be created during the making and preparation procedure, and as much as possible needs to be removed both from the work and, wherever possible, from the surrounding atmosphere before any finishing is carried out. Most painters carry a dust brush in their back pocket and give the immediate working area a quick going over to ensure their work is given a chance.

Unless you have a vacuum cleaner hooked up to your power tools, and an ambient filter running 24/7, it is likely that there will still be a lot of airborne dust around. Many painters use a tack cloth; a thin rag impregnated with a resinous oil, making it faintly sticky to the touch and just the thing to pick up every last little bit of dust and debris it comes into contact with.

There's no avoiding dust in preparation (above) but a quick going over with the vacuum will help (below left).

A tack cloth is cheap and very useful.

The working area can be isolated by a dust guard like this one.

Where would we be without masking tape?

Masking

Not everyone is blessed with a steady hand and nerves of steel, and when it comes to painting a straight line, you could undoubtedly benefit from having a roll or two of masking tape in your kit. Masking tape has many uses in general woodwork and I am never without a roll whenever I go out on a job; if nothing else it will bandage up any cuts efficiently – and cheaply too!

There's something very satisfying about setting out a dividing line on a wall, say at dado height, masking it up, applying a couple of coats of emulsion, then carefully peeling the tape off to reveal a perfectly straight line. I find masking tape to be a great help when painting skirting boards for example, or the base of a piece of fitted furniture where a fitted carpet butts up to it.

I do draw the line, however, at masking up the glass in a wooden window frame – the effort it takes to get the tape on neatly, especially in the corners,

outweighs the time 'saved' on conventional cutting in. Cutting in is an acquired skill, and requires a calm mind and a steady hand. A straight line is the objective and the bristle tips the means of achieving it. Just don't be in too much of a hurry and you'll be all right. If you do use masking tape, make sure you remove it as soon as possible. If tape is left on a window for longer than a day or two – even less if it's sunny – it can be a real pain to remove and you'll end up damaging all your good paintwork.

Masking tape can make a painting job easier – just be sure to remove it soon after.

Application

Brush strokes can be used to emphasize joinery.

The tips of the bristles lay the paint off nicely.

Paint should be applied with light, firm strokes, and restraint shown in its application. The important thing to remember is to 'lay off' the paint that has been already applied, that is, to lightly brush the work with the tips of the bristles to flat it off and give it uniformity. Laying off should generally be in the direction of grain or moulding, or simply in the longest or most natural orientation. This is where a good brush will pay dividends, as one with soft and fine bristles will leave a smoother finish and better appearance than a cheap, coarsely bristled one.

Give a bit of thought to the painting process before you start and, when faced with a piece of furniture or household woodwork, don't just steam in at the nearest part to you, or the top left hand corner, for instance – it really will make a difference if you follow a few basic principles. We've probably all seen the diagram of the panelled door, so let's just have another look at it, but this time consider just why area 1 should be done first, and area 9 last.

As you progress across a freshly prepared surface with your brush and paint, the first part covered will be drying, while the most recent part will still be wet. As long as you continue to apply more paint in the region of this 'wet edge', things will be fine, and it will all blend in nicely. However, you can come unstuck when you return to an earlier, dry-ish part of the job and find that the wet paint you've just applied is dragging at the nearly dry stuff, making an ugly and perceptible join.

This is the recommended order for painting a door.

Paint can create a stunning effect.

If we were to start at the top left-hand corner of the door and progress downwards and across, we would soon have too many wet edges to cope with. The result would be rough joins on stiles and panels, especially if the weather is hot and the paint is drying even more quickly than usual. By following the pro-painter's scheme for the door, you will soon find that each area can be safely tackled in its entirety, and any meeting of dry and wet edges will be naturally disguised in the joinery of the door itself. Don't just take my word for it, have a go yourself and you'll soon see what I mean.

But furniture can often be a different matter, especially when there are many areas or components to consider, such as on a chair for example. When it comes to carcassed furniture, like cupboards, wardrobes or chests, it's fairly straightforward to address each side, panel or rail individually. Apply the principles used in the door example described previously, and you should be all right. Wherever possible, be sure to remove doors and drawers and if you can take a drawer front off, this will definitely help you to get even better results.

A chair, or other legged piece, is one of the hardest things to paint with a brush, and I would have to say

it's worth considering a spray job, which is often the easiest, although maybe not the cheapest, option (see chapter 2:6). All I can suggest for the brush approach is to start on the 'inside' of the job, i.e. those areas that are furthest away from you or hardest to reach. This way you will slowly work your way 'out' and are less likely to spoil the earlier parts of the job.

If you have prepared, primed and undercoated your work well, you may find that just a single top coat will suffice. However, for a truly successful finish, you should rub down the job – when the last coat is perfectly dry – with a fine paper, dust it off and apply a second coat to finish. Not only will this give the work more protection and a better appearance, but your hand on the second coat will be guided by what you have learned on the previous one, and any tricky areas can be identified and dealt with more effectively. This leads to a finer finish and satisfaction all round which is, after all, what it's all about.

KEY POINT

It can be tricky sometimes, but if fittings such as handles and escutcheons can be unscrewed, then it's worth making that little bit of extra effort; but just make sure you mark them so that you know what goes where. Getting the hinges mixed up can actually make a difference to how a door closes, so use a wax pencil or similar to identify one from another.

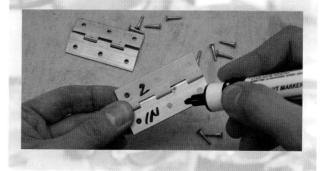

2.9 Special effects

Fashions come and go, and nowhere – apart from high street boutiques and clothes shops – is this more evident than in our homes. It only takes a small clique of celebrity designers to talk up a new 'look' or fad, then a mention or two on a popular daytime TV show, and before long we're all scumbling our walls or stencilling our furniture. It's likely there's a completely new fad even now, displacing chintz or minimalism as the next 'big thing', and doing all it can to have us rushing for the interiors magazines and anxiously poring over paint charts and fabric swatches.

Well, this is modern life for us, and just one more reason why many of us feel the need to get creative with our woodwork tools and make or renovate items for the home ourselves. When it comes to finishing, it's nice to occasionally break out of the customary expectations of the standard shiny finish, and go for something a bit different. Here then, are one or two finishes which may be worth considering. Treat this chapter as a kind of overview for specialist finishes; some further research or professional guidance is recommended for most of these.

Liming

Liming gives a light feel to these built-in oak bookcases.

Liming is a finish that has been in use for centuries. Simply stated, it consists of rubbing lime or chalk paste into the wood and is most effective when used on open-grained timbers like oak. The overall effect is one of lightening the work, as well as giving an instant impression of age or venerability, and can look good both on large areas, such as panelling, and on small pieces of standard domestic furniture. The actual process is straightforward enough, but does involve a fair bit of elbow grease, so be prepared to break a sweat during the job. Your timber should be prepared as per normal for finishing, but it is advisable to open the grain a bit more where required, by means of a firm going over with a fine wire brush. Test it out on a sample or two before attempting the actual job.

Once the surface has been satisfactorily prepared, dust the work off, and apply your chosen liming compound. Rub it into the grain with a rag, making sure to wipe off the excess before it dries. Generally available in paste or wax form, the main difference between the liming compounds is that liming wax is marginally easier to apply, and needs little further finishing, bar an optional extra coat of a regular wax polish. If you intend to polish or varnish your work for extra protection, a liming paste will permit this, and if you can't find a suitable paste, you can make your own substitute with white undercoat paint, thinned a little with white spirit. Just be sure to clean it off fairly quickly. If you take your time and experiment a bit first, a very good effect can be achieved. When used on a large job, for example a staircase, liming can really lighten things up while still retaining all the beauty of the wood grain.

A preliminary wire brushing is recommended.

Rub liming paste into and across the grain.

Ebonizing

Popular in late Victorian and early Edwardian times, and often combined with gold leaf accents, properly executed ebonizing can create a really dramatic look on any special furniture or fitted work. Ebonizing was originally conceived during the Regency period (circa 1820) as a means of simulating expensive and hard to obtain exotic timbers; it was soon taken up as a fashion of its day, and has remained popular ever since.

It's one of those jobs that must be done well to achieve the full effect; otherwise you may as well just slap on some black gloss paint. For this reason, ebonizing won't work on just any old timber, but needs to be applied to close-grained hardwoods such as mahogany and walnut, or lighter timbers like maple and beech. If you're in doubt, consider grain-filling (see chapter 1:2) before going any further. Once the piece is prepared, it needs to be stained black. Ebonite polish is spirit-based, so your stain should be either water- or oil-based so as not to be pulled off when the polish goes on. Make sure you leave it to dry thoroughly, and lightly rub down any grain that may have been raised if a water-based stain has been used. Ebonite or black French polish is

The work should be stained black before applying ebonite polish.

generally only available at specialist suppliers, and a bit of leg work may be necessary to track some down.

Applying the polish is a similar technique to French polishing (see chapter 2:2), only somewhat blacker. For this reason it's best not to use your regular rubber or mop brush as these will remain contaminated forever, regardless of how thoroughly you clean up afterwards. If you can afford it, I would recommend the purchase of another mop brush for the first coat. This should be slightly thinned and then rubbed down with a fine paper when dry. It's then just a case of applying further coats with a dedicated rubber until you have sufficient polish on the job, usually about three or four coats. Shellac polish takes a day or two to fully harden, and it's best to wait this long before the final step in the process which is a wire and wax with 000 or 0000 grade wire wool and a dark paste wax of your choice.

Be sure to rub down between coats.

Gilding

Golden furniture: the ultimate luxury.

Gilding is the general term used for applying metal leaf of all kinds, although most of us will think of gold before silver or bronze. It is a highly skilled technique and one that requires considerable practice before tackling any large areas. It's also worth considering the aesthetic value of gilt work before you begin, so visit some stately homes and museums to get an idea of its effectiveness.

Gold of the highest purity is traditionally used – typically 23 or 24 carat – and it is rolled and beaten flat to cover 250sq ft per oz (76.2sq m per 28g). The gold is then cut into 3½in (89mm) squares, 1oz (28g) yielding 2,500 squares, and these are packaged up into booklets of 25 pages or leaves. Each leaf of gold is inserted between pages of thin paper which have been dusted to prevent the gold from sticking.

Particular care must be taken in preparation: for the gold leaf to look its best, the surface must be filled and primed to a very high standard. Gold leaf requires no glue as such, but a liquid called gold size is carefully applied to the surface. As this is oil-based, the prepared surface must be impervious to prevent it soaking in. To prevent the leaf from sticking to any of the surrounding parts, these need be dusted with

French chalk or given a coat of glair (made by beating one egg white in a pint of water). The gold size dries to leave the surface faintly tacky; this will remain so for a number of days as the work progresses.

A professional gilder will keep the leaf in a cushion – a small upholstered board – sheltered behind a draught screen to stop it blowing away. The leaf is prepared and transferred into place by means of a long-bladed knife and various sable brushes, then dabbed down and burnished with a pad of cotton wool.

All in all it's a tricky operation, and I'd recommend starting off with one of the booklets of metal leaf (sometimes known as 'Dutch leaf'). These are designed for easier application and can be laid straight from the page with a suitable soft brush. When gilding larger areas, care should be taken on joints to avoid the appearance of a 'grid' effect. If a good quality leaf has been used then no further treatment or coating is needed, as this will only tarnish and spoil the effect.

A professional gilder's tool kit.

Fuming

Fuming is not the most widely used of finishes, but is still considered by many furniture makers to be worthy of the effort, imparting as it does an even, natural-looking colour that is hard to imitate with stains. A chemical reaction occurs when some timbers, most notably oak, are exposed to ammonia vapours, causing the wood to darken. It's hard to describe, but a fumed colour looks subtly but attractively different to a simple stain of the same shade, and will penetrate deeper into the wood. It is a finish that seems to suit Arts and Crafts furniture particularly well.

Ammonia is a highly stringent and volatile chemical, once the base of 'smelling salts', and is still used by antique restorers and fakers. It was extremely popular with bank robbers in the 1970s before it was withdrawn from public sale. It can still be acquired legitimately, but do expect a bit of bureaucracy first. Fuming is simple enough, but it does necessitate the use of an enclosed space or suitable structure known as a fume cupboard, in the case of an actual wooden structure, or a tent, as the temporary version is known. The items or components are placed in the cupboard with a shallow tray of liquid ammonia. The door is closed and the work left to the fumes, usually for a number of hours. Once your work is suitably darkened, leave it to air for a day or two before applying the finish of your choice.

Ammonia is a fierce corrosive and the fumes will attack metal with gusto. Often used in the antiques trade to simulate age on brasswork; I once accidentally left a brass cupboard lock to fume all night and watched with dismay when it fell to pieces the next morning. It's advisable to check now and again that everything's all right.

The oak desk tidy on the right has been fumed.

A simple fuming tent constructed from polythene sheeting.

Ammonia fumes will readily corrode brass fittings.

125

Paint

Paint can be used imaginatively in many ways, from rich lacquers, delicate decorations and even faux graining to simulate exotic timbers themselves. It's far from unusual to see a piece of old furniture sitting outside a second-hand shop with a spectacular or unlikely wood grain adorning its prominent surfaces. Quite often there'll be a small light patch that is painfully apparent, and this is where someone has started to strip the piece, only to discover that the grain is actually a paint effect, or even stuck on.

Hand-painted decoration.

An elaborate bureau in Japanese lacquer.

This is how cheap stuff was 'improved' in days gone by, and, as long as the surface was protected by varnish, would give a good account of itself and look for all the world like top quality hardwood. Realistic graining is an exceptional skill, primarily a master painter and decorator's art, and a far cry from the botched efforts one often sees on TV makeover shows. Graining has traditionally been used to enhance cheaper timbers, and it is an effect that will last successfully for many years, requiring only a little touching up from time to time and the occasional fresh coat of varnish.

A blank, end-of-terrace wall is enlivened by skilful use of paint.

It is a gradual process, and requires the usual surface preparation, followed by the application of a suitable base colour – a deep red brown for mahogany, a pale mid-brown for oak and so on. A thinnish mixture of a darker coloured paint, oil and turps is laid over and manipulated with various combs, brushes and rags to simulate the desired timber grain. With a good knowledge of wood grains, and sufficient care and practice, a very pleasing effect can be created, but it can easily look false if too great an area is attempted or more than one piece of woodwork is treated.

Similar techniques can also be attempted with polish and spirit colours to enhance an otherwise dull piece of timber on say, a panel or the side of a carcass. It's quite common to see this effect on piano cases or wardrobes of the mid-20th century.

A pair of artfully grained doors, if slightly worn.

ⓘTECHNIQUE:

Simple graining

A warm-toned semi-gloss base coat.

A 'scumble' mixture is laid over.

Rubber combs simulate grain.

A rocker can create 'heart' wood.

Bleaching

Standard household bleach has little effect.

Two-part bleach is the most efficient.

Successive applications will turn this timber white.

Bleach comes in many different strengths, from household to industrial, depending on requirements. Where the weaker types may bleach out stains, dyes and ink blots, to actually lighten the wood itself requires a more serious treatment. Most polishers will prefer to use oxalic acid for minor blemishes, which can be mixed up from powder and needs to be brushed on and left overnight to be really effective.

When it comes to lightening timber, the most effective bleach has to be the two-part variety. It comes in two bottles, usually marked A and B, and is mixed on the timber itself, part B being added a few minutes after part A. The resulting cocktail is the strongest bleach that you can easily buy and, depending on the type of wood, can produce dramatic results. Because the whole process is not an exact science, results cannot be relied upon for consistency or even coloration. Only a great deal of practice and experience will tell you just what you might expect, but as usual it really does pay to experiment first.

Whatever chemical you do employ however, just be sure to wash the work down thoroughly with water and a coarse cloth or brush to clean off any crystalline residue before continuing with your next stage of the job.

Faking age

Genuine age is appreciated by all.

Without a doubt this has to be the hardest special finish of all. It takes more than five minutes spent beating a table with a piece of chain and speckling it with some black stain to make a piece of furniture look old. If you're looking to enhance a piece of 'period' furniture you've just made, then a bit of ageing could be considered appropriate but be careful, as it's very easy to get wrong and can often end up looking ridiculous.

If you've got your heart set on a finish of this type then first you must study your subject, which will involve regular trips to museums, galleries and antique shops. One of the reasons antique furniture has been popular for many years is the indefinable look that an old piece slowly acquires through time. We talk of the surface patina as the most obvious characteristic that a table or chair may have developed, but there are also more subtle indicators of age that the eye picks up and the brain only subconsciously registers. We all know that wood moves and settles over time, and this, along with with physical wear and tear, greatly contributes to the overall appearance.

These then are just some of the things to consider when embarking on a spot of fakery, but we should really only concern ourselves here with the finish. You'll be looking at a wax or a French polished finish, but the work really starts with the colour. Any professional finisher will agree that getting the colour right is probably the hardest part of any job, and requires a good eye and plenty of practice. I can't add much more except my standard line of 'lots of practice, trial and error', which really is a thorough, albeit painful, way to learn.

Make a study of antiques before trying to imitate them.

Part 3
Projects

3.1 Waxed box

This simple pine box made a nice subject for a straightforward seal and wax job. To be assured of a successful outcome though, the usual policy of thorough preparations should still be adhered to. These can start before you get to the finishing stage, and will undoubtedly prove to be worth the trouble. Pine is a good subject for a wax finish, the muted sheen tending to suit this timber possibly more than any other.

1 Start the cleaning up early in the job, especially on those parts that will be hard to access later on.

2 Once completed, the job should be given a final sanding. Here I went down to 240 grit.

3 The box is given a good dust-off, followed by a wipe over with a tack cloth.

4 The job should be dismantled, and all the brasswork removed.

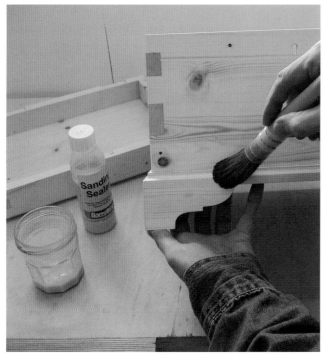

5 A coat of sanding sealer is applied with a mop brush. This will ensure the stain will take more uniformly.

6 A water-based stain is applied with a sponge brush and then wiped off with a rag.

7 This leaves a nice antique pine colour.

8 After a quick flick over with a fine abrasive paper, a coat of button polish is applied.

9 Another light sanding prepares the box for the final finish.

10 A good quality paste wax is rubbed into the grain with a rag.

11 The wax is left to dry for half an hour, then buffed up to a pleasing shine.

3.2 Restoring a front door

Painting a front door is a fairly straightforward job but one that will really benefit from the time and effort put into preparation and execution. This particular door was in a pretty rough state, primarily down to its seaside location and top-of-street position. The fact that it faced south and was very close to the sea meant the door was constantly exposed to serious weathering, and both the paint and the very fabric of the door itself had suffered since it was first hung, about 170 years ago.

2 The first task is to remove all of the fittings, which is often a challenge when there is so much corrosion involved.

1 The original state of the door: about ten years after its last paint job.

3 The panels on this door were badly cracked and had been filled with a variety of mediums, including newspaper and putty.

4 All loose filler should be removed and the woodwork made good where possible. Here a padsaw is being used to clear out the filler from the cracks.

5 It is apparent that something more than decorator's filler will be required for this door.

6 Thin strips of wood, known as fillets, have been run off on a tablesaw and glued
with expanding PU glue into the cracks.

7 While the glue is setting, all other loose paint, filler and debris can be scraped off
and chipped out.

8 Once the glue has dried, the fillets can be planed in flush with the door panels.

9 The whole door is then given a coarse sanding to remove any final bits of loose paint, and to provide a good key for the next coat. Even with a door of this age and condition, it's rarely necessary to have to resort to burning off the old paint with a torch.

11 Any new or exposed timber and filler should be primed before undercoating.

10 Use a good quality exterior filler, leave to dry and then sand down flush with the surrounding surfaces. Since discovering it many years ago, I now use only Toupret, a French filler which mixes up into a creamy smooth consistency and is a dream to sand down.

12 A suitably coloured undercoat is applied. On a job like this, which you want to last as long as possible, it's really worth using top quality exterior paints.

13 The job should be sanded down between coats. Use a block whenever possible, which will improve the flatness of the final coat.

14 Two top coats later, the job is finished. Not only has its appearance been hugely improved, but now the door somehow seems more solid, secure and imposing than before.

3.3 Spraying a table top

There are times when a spray job is the only answer for a piece of furniture, and this simple table top in oak-veneered MDF was a prime example. A lacquer finish can be readily applied in a relatively short time and a job such as this one should only take a couple of hours at the most.

As ever, preparation is vital for success, so be sure to sand your work down to at least a 240 grit grade, preferably finer. Your spraying area should be isolated where possible, with adequate extraction on hand. Protective clothing must be worn, and an efficient mask is an absolute necessity. Although a fully enclosed, self-contained mask and visor with its own air supply is the best choice, the 3M mask I'm wearing for this project proved to be very effective, so much so that I couldn't even detect a whiff of thinners throughout the job.

1 Good preparation is everything in a finishing job, not least where spraying is involved.

2 Make sure your work is free from dust. Use a brush followed by a tack cloth.

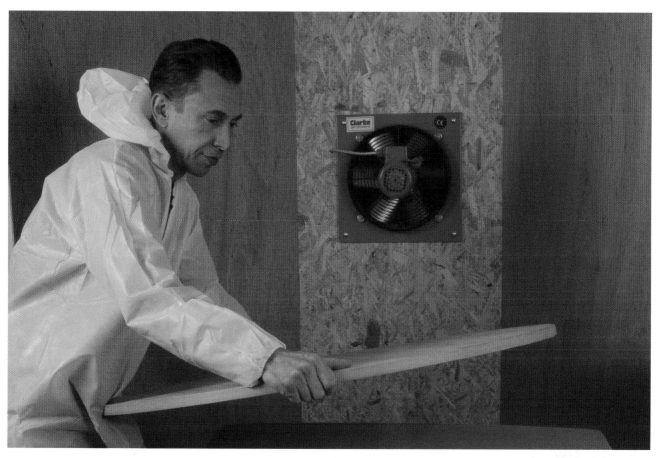

3 A piece of cardboard protects the 'A' side of the work from damage while the first seal coat goes on.

4 Better results are obtained with many thin coats rather than one or two thick ones. Here I'm thinning the lacquer by about 40%. The whole process is sensitive to local temperature and humidity conditions, so a test spraying is advised.

5 It's always a sound policy to keep any furniture top 'balanced' by treating both sides alike. My first coat is on the underside of the top and will effectively seal it as well as providing a bit more practice before the real thing.

6 Try and maintain a constant distance from the job, and start and finish spraying off the workpiece, overlapping each 'line' or pass.

7 As soon as each coat is dry – which should only be five or ten minutes – sand it down with a fine stearate-impregnated paper. If the surface shows any sign of texturing, or an orange peel effect, now is the time to sand it flat with the aid of a block and thin your lacquer a bit more before the next application.

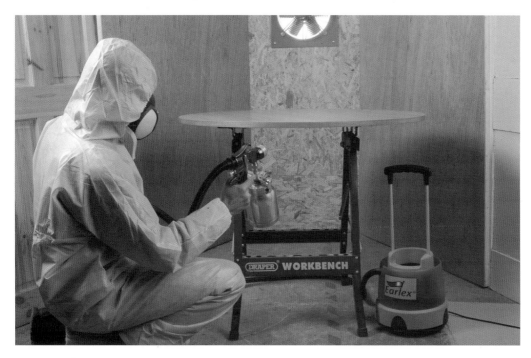

8 Start by spraying the edge of the table top. Direct the spray from beneath so as to avoid overspray on the main surface.

9 The top can now be addressed. Maintain a uniform height from the surface, and track across the top in parallel strokes, overlapping each one by about half, and spraying past the edge each time.

10 Successive coats can now be applied, making sure to rub down each one in between. This table ended up with four coats, which was easily enough.

11 Be sure to clean all of your spray kit thoroughly, and make sure the gun is clean inside and out. To ensure it won't be blocked when you next come to use it, spray a fair amount of thinners through it to clean the nozzle and inner parts.

12 Leave the job to harden off overnight, and give it a careful check over the next day. It should be perfectly fine and ready to go, but, depending on spray-room conditions – most notably extraction – it might be slightly rough to the touch. This will be due to settling of 'over-spray' dust, and can be smoothed off by a coating of paste wax applied with some 0000 wire wool. Finally, a vigorous buffing will bring the finish up a treat, and will enhance the smooth feel of the lacquer too.

13 The finished job, now part of a light and modern suite.

3.4 Side table

I made this table from an assortment of reclaimed mahogany, and as a result it needed a good finish job to both harmonize the timbers and to suit its period design. Inspired by a method pioneered by American expert Michael Dresdner, I went for a colour build of two stains and a tinted grain filler, followed by a French polish finish which I felt the style demanded.

After some thorough preparation, I spread the work out over three days, mainly to give the stain a good chance to dry (it was pretty cold out in our workshop). I would suggest that you allow this sort of time frame for any similar job. The end result was pretty good, and has so far met with universal acclaim.

1 The unfinished table, ready for staining and polishing.

2 All components should be separated for individual treatment.

3 After final sanding, dust each piece down well . . .

4 . . . and wipe over with a tack cloth.

5 Prepare samples, make your plans before you start – and stick to them.

6 Mask off where necessary.

7 Begin staining from the 'inside' out.

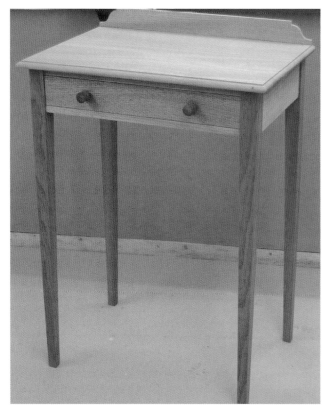

8 The first stain coat is left to dry.

9 The second colour coat is applied like the first.

10 Apply the stain briskly and wipe off the excess straight away.

11 Grain filler is firmly rubbed in with a rag.

12 It is then left briefly . . .

13 . . . and vigorously rubbed off again.

14 The grain filler both colours the job and prepares for the next stage.

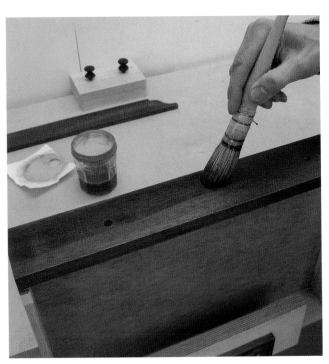

16 Watch out for runs on edges and corners.

15 A thin brush coat of polish is carefully applied with a mop brush.

17 Use long, straight strokes to lay the polish onto the top.

18 When dry, rub down with a fine paper.

19 Wipe off each surface thoroughly before the next coat.

20 The second coat of polish is applied with a rubber.

21 Use firm positive pressure for the top.

22 The next day, the table is waxed . . .

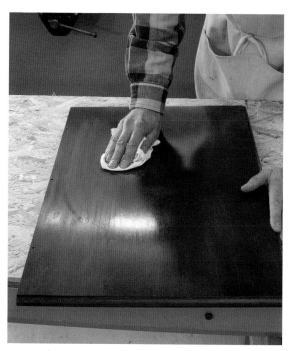

23 . . . and then buffed off to the final finish.

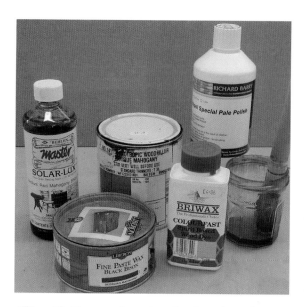

24 The products involved in the job: two stains, grain filler, Special Pale French polish, paste wax.

25 The finished result, well worth the effort.

Suitable finishes for popular timbers

Timber	Characteristics	Treatment	Suitability
Pine	Softwood, readily available	Stain	Prone to blotching. A light application of sanding sealer is required first, particularly on end grain
		French polish	Best used as a seal prior to waxing
		Briwax	Good, no sealer required
		Paste wax	OK, but will need coat of sanding sealer or spirit-based varnish first
		Varnish, oil-based	Good, but wears quickly on floors, so multiple coats required. Avoid coloured variety
		Varnish, acrylic	Good, but can look a bit pale in colour
		Oil	Absorbency means more coats will be required. Hard to avoid it looking a bit flat
		Lacquer	As a softwood it is particularly susceptible to chipping
		Special treatments	Classic timber for Briwax. Can be 'aged' with caustic soda, but wash down well afterwards
		Paint	Good, but be sure to treat any knots or resinous areas first. Primer recommended
Oak	Hardwood, open grained	Stain	Takes all stains well
		French polish	Will polish up nicely, but forget about a full-grain finish
		Briwax	OK but it doesn't do the wood justice
		Paste wax	OK, but disappointing without sealer coat. Requires patience to achieve a satisfying finish
		Varnish, oil-based	OK. Any external varnish coat must be maintained as discoloration is swift and hard to reverse
		Varnish, acrylic	OK, but bland areas of straight grain will benefit from staining first
		Floor seal	Suitable. Acrylic seals will give a pale result, oil-based seals will produce a richer tone
		Oil	Suitable for all oils
		Lacquer	Suitable for all lacquers
		Special treatments	Prime candidate for liming and fuming
		Paint	Not advisable
Walnut	Hardwood, close grained	Stain	Takes all stains well
		French polish	Will take a polish extremely well, with or without grain filler
		Briwax	Deserves better
		Paste wax	Only as maintenance
		Varnish, oil-based	This timber will look great under anything
		Varnish, acrylic	See above
		Floor seal	Suitable. Acrylic seals will give a pale result; oil-based seals will give a richer tone
		Oil	Suitable for all oils
		Lacquer	Suitable for all lacquers
		Special treatments	If you've got the patience, naturally coloured walnut mellows down beautifully over the years
		Paint	Don't do it!
Mahogany	Hardwood, close grained	Stain	Stains pretty well, but watch out for any areas of short grain
		French polish	Ideal candidate, but may well need grain-filling
		Briwax	It will wax, but just doesn't look right

Timber	Characteristics	Treatment	Suitability
Mahogany		Paste wax	Only as maintenance
		Varnish, oil-based	Best restricted to yacht-varnish aboard ship
		Varnish, acrylic	I wouldn't if I were you
		Floor seal	Oil-based seal is most suitable
		Oil	Suitable for all oils
		Lacquer	Suitable for all lacquers
		Special treatments	Will ebonize well. Older, reclaimed timber is preferable for both figure and colour
		Paint	Only if you really have to
Maple	Blond hardwood	Stain	Prone to blotching. A light application of sanding sealer is required, particularly on end grain
		French polish	Fine, this is where the true capabilities of coloured polish can be seen
		Briwax	OK; can end up looking patchy
		Paste wax	OK; sealer coat is recommended
		Varnish, oil-based	OK; will show brush marks very readily
		Varnish, acrylic	OK; can look extremely pale
		Floor seal	An acrylic seal on this timber will give you a very light-coloured floor indeed
		Oil	Good for all oils
		Lacquer	OK, no problem
		Special treatments	Its fine, close grain makes it suitable for many treatments
		Paint	If you feel you have to
Beech	Relatively cheap, popular hardwood, sometimes pink	Stain	Takes a stain pretty well, but not the best option
		French polish	Not usually done
		Briwax	OK
		Paste wax	OK, but seal first
		Varnish, oil-based	OK
		Varnish, acrylic	Leaves it looking a bit washed out
		Floor seal	OK
		Oil	Fair, best on kitchen items and toys
		Lacquer	OK
		Special treatments	Beech is a robust timber that will put up with pretty much anything
		Paint	Good, so why not?
Ash	Pale hardwood with pronounced grain	Stain	Care must be taken here to get the most out of the contrasting grain
		French polish	Takes it well enough
		Briwax	OK, but can become patchy
		Paste wax	Builds up nicely
		Varnish, oil-based	No problem
		Varnish, acrylic	OK, but the wood should be stained first to get maximum effect
		Floor seal	Fine; use an oil-based one if you don't want to stain the wood first
		Oil	Linseed is recommended for a warm golden glow
		Lacquer	OK
		Special treatments	Despite the noticeable grain pattern it looks good ebonized
		Paint	Pronounced grain pattern spoils the painted look
Cherry	Hardwood, American species very popular	Stain	Prone to blotching; light application of sanding sealer is required, particularly on end grain.
		French polish	Not bad. Semi-matt is best.

Suitable finishes for popular timbers

Timber	Characteristics	Treatment	Suitability
Cherry		Briwax	OK
		Paste wax	OK; use sealer first
		Varnish, oil-based	Not recommended, but takes OK
		Varnish, acrylic	Not recommended, but not too bad
		Floor seal	Will assist the darkening process
		Oil	Fair
		Lacquer	OK
		Special treatments	Cherry will naturally darken quickly on exposure to daylight, so best left unstained
		Paint	Don't do it
Birch-faced ply	Man-made board, top quality, made from North European hardwood	Stain	Prone to blotching, light application of sanding sealer required, watch out for patches
		French polish	Not really suitable
		Briwax	OK
		Paste wax	OK; sealer is recommended first
		Varnish, oil-based	OK; use to warm up colour tone
		Varnish, acrylic	OK; use to keep colour pale
		Floor seal	No problem
		Oil	It won't look its best, remaining flat and dirty-looking
		Lacquer	Fine
		Special treatments	Colour looks best left natural or non-wood primary (such as blue and red)
		Paint	Don't buy the most expensive man-made board, then paint it
Far Eastern ply	Man-made board, cheap, made from East Asian hardwood	Stain	Rarely looks good, will blotch. Glue often has seeped through
		French polish	Will look bad and would need maximum grain-filling first
		Briwax	A quick shortcut to nowhere
		Paste wax	Only on top of grain filler and seal
		Varnish, oil-based	Three coats is minimum
		Varnish, acrylic	Three coats is minimum
		Floor seal	OK, but watch out for splinters
		Oil	Disappointing
		Lacquer	OK
		Special treatments	Avoid wherever possible
		Paint	Recommended
MDF	The all-round man-made board	Stain	Use oil stains where possible; seal the edges first
		French polish	Just don't admit to it
		Briwax	Nasty
		Paste wax	Seal first, but don't expect a high shine
		Varnish, oil-based	OK
		Varnish, acrylic	OK
		Floor seal	OK; repair it quickly if the finish gets chipped to prevent moisture access
		Oil	OK, but you'll need more than you expected
		Lacquer	Fine
		Special treatments	Not the best material for a timber finish, but does well once veneered
		Paint	Now you're talking

Glossary

A

A & B
A two-part powerful bleach for timber.

Acrylic
In finishing terms, acrylic means water-based.

Alkyd
Synthetic resin, much used in finishing products, made by reacting alcohol with an acid.

Aniline
Chemical originally used in the production of the first dyes. The term is broadly applied to all soluble synthetic wood dyes.

B

Base
The liquid which allows the finishing product to be evenly applied. Always evaporates. Most commonly mineral spirits (oil), alcohol (spirit), water (acrylic).

Burnish
Physical compression of wood pores which flattens and smoothes, thus creating a sheen.

C

Carrier
see Base.

Catalyst
An element which speeds up a process without affecting it in any other way.

Chemical stain
Reacts with other chemicals naturally present in the wood to produce a change in colour. Includes bichromate of potash and ammonia.

D

Denatured alcohol
Pure alcohol (ethanol) which has had chemicals added to it to prevent human consumption.

De-nib
Removing the roughness left after a new coat of polish or varnish by lightly sanding with fine abrasive paper.

Drier
Liquid metal-based chemical which is added to reactive finishes to speed up drying.

Dye
Coloured chemical dissolved in a carrier.

E

Emulsion
A mixture of two substances (usually liquid) which would not normally mix but do, thanks to the introduction of an emulsifier which prevents them separating.

Evaporative finish
That which forms a film coating by means of the base or carrier completely evaporating, no other physical or chemical reaction taking place. Such a finish can be redissolved by its solvent at any time, such as shellac and some lacquers.

F

Fad
As in 'fadding up', the initial method of quickly bodying up a shellac finish with a crude pad prior to employing the rubber.

Finish
Any protective or decorative coating applied as a liquid or gel.

Flammable
Will readily burn; has a flash point (i.e. when it will catch fire) of below 100°F (37.8°C).

French polish
Originally the name given to the shellac and alcohol mixture; now applies to the method too.

Glossary

G

Glaze
Colour applied between coats of clear finish.

J

Japan colours
Pigments ground in fast-drying oil, most popularly red or black.

L

Lacquer
A finish that dries by solvent evaporation only.

M

Mineral spirits
Petroleum distillate used as solvent and diluting agent; e.g. white spirit.

N

Naptha
Similar to white spirit, but slightly oilier. Most commonly used as base for stains.

Non-combustible
Substance that won't ignite at any temperature.

Non-flammable
Substance that won't ignite below 100°F (37.8°C).

O

Orange peel
Undesirable rough texture in a sprayed finish, usually caused by too thick a mixture.

Over-spray
Gritty texture caused by spray droplets drying in the air before coming to rest.

Oxalic acid
Wood bleach and powder crystals mixed with water. Good for tannin stains on oak.

P

Pigment
Any dry mineral that can be added to a coating, stain or filler.

Polyurethane
General term for the majority of resins used in both oil- and water-based finishes.

Primer
A sealer coat which also improves adhesion between the substrate and further coatings.

Pull over
The act of applying a finish by hand with a rubber; often a way of improving an otherwise ordinary job.

Pumice
Finely ground volcanic rock that can be used as an abrasive to knock a gloss back to satin.

R

Reactive
A finish that works by other means than purely solvent evaporation, generally polymerization, such as oil-based varnish, linseed oil.

Relative humidity
Measurement of moisture in air. Warm air holds more water than cold.

Resin
The solid part of a varnish. Can be natural (such as rosin, amber) or synthetic (such as urethane).

Rubbing compound
Very fine abrasive paste used for final polish – on lacquer, for example.

S

Sealer
Purpose-made liquid finish designed to dry fast, build quickly and sand easily. Essential on porous grains and MDF.

Shellac

Liquid finish made from insect-derived resins dissolved in alcohol.

Solvent

Any material that will dissolve a dried finish.

Stain

Something that will change the colour of a wood without obscuring the grain.

Stearate

Zinc-based chemical added to fine sandpaper to reduce clogging. Also used in sanding sealer.

T

Thixotropic

At rest the product is thick or gel-like, but when energy is applied by brushing or wiping, it converts to a liquid state.

V

Viscosity

The measure of a liquid's resistance to flow, simply determined by how thick it is. A viscosity cup is used to determine if a product needs thinning prior to being sprayed.

W

Wiping finish

A combination of oil and varnish in an easy to apply form.

Y

Yacht varnish

Oil-based varnish designed for exterior use. Traditional yacht varnish is made from tung oil and synthetic resin; slow to dry but flexible and long-lasting with natural UV resistance.

Acknowledgements

After what seems like 20 years this book is finally finished, and I'd like to thank my family, friends and colleagues in putting up with me for the entire duration. Technical help from Mark Poulter, Ronnie Rustin and Eddie Fitch has been gratefully received and a big thank you is also due to Michael Dresdner who has inspired me through his writings. Finally, stalwarts Anthony Bailey (photography) and Ralph Laughton (general advice), who have kept me going, are also due a shout.

Manufacturers

UK

Axminster, safety, general kit	www.axminster.co.uk
Barrettine, finishes	www.barrettine.co.uk
Behlen, finishes	www.behlen.co.uk
Bollom (for Briwax)	www.bollom.com
Clarke (compressors and fans)	www.clarkeinternational.com
CSM AbrasivesPlus	www.abrasivesplus.com
DeVilbiss, spray equipment	www.devilbiss-spraysite.co.uk
Dustguard (room sealer)	www.dustguard.co.uk
Morrells, stains and finishes	www.morrells-woodfinishes.com
Osmo, oil	www.osmouk.com
Richard Barry, finishing supplies	www.richardbarry.co.uk
Ronseal, varnishes	www.ronseal.co.uk
Rustins, finishes	www.rustins.co.uk
Sadolin, woodcoatings	www.sadolin.co.uk
Tom Faulkner, metal furniture	www.tomfaulkner.co.uk
Trend, face masks	www.trendmachinery.co.uk

USA

Benjamin Moore, paints	www.benjaminmoore.com
Samuel Cabot Inc, stains	www.cabotstain.com
Flecto, varnishes, floor seals	www.flecto.com
Gemini, stains, preservatives	www.geminicoatings.com
WD Lockwood, stains	www.wdlockwood.com
Minwax, lacquers, waxes	www.minwax.com
Waterlox, oils	www.waterlox.com
Zinsser, paints and sealers	www.zinsser.com

Index

Index

About the author

Mark Cass was born in Russian Poland in 1857, and passed his childhood in the shadow of revolution. At the age of seventeen he went to Marseille to become an apprentice in the merchant marine which began a long period of adventure at sea. He became a British subject in 1886, and three years later settled in London where he became interested in ancient Greek theology.

It was during research in Cyprus that he met up with the man who was to change his life, the philosopher Aristophanes, who convinced him that his practical talents were languishing under an avalanche of historical exploration. Returning to Britain he became a virtual recluse for six years as he struggled to master the art of wood finishing, finally emerging back into the public spotlight with his now famous Light and Shade exhibition. The success of the show led to many lucrative contracts, and he went on to found the Blue Cross brand of products which continue to sell globally today.

Now retired, Mark Cass spends his time collecting cardboard and gazing at the sky.

Note from the Publishers:
The Publishers choose to neither deny nor substantiate the autobiography supplied by the author. In the interest of open disclosure and publishing integrity they feel bound to inform the general readership of a person known to them, also going by the name of Mark Cass, who is Editor of *New Woodworking* magazine, with nearly 25 years' practical experience in the woodworking and building trades.

Guild of Master Craftsman Publications,
Castle Place, 166 High Street, Lewes,
East Sussex BN7 1XU, United Kingdom
Tel: 01273 488005 Fax: 01273 402866
Website: www.thegmcgroup.com

Contact us for a complete catalogue, or visit our website.
Orders by credit card are accepted.